Diana's Diary

Diana's Diary

AN INTIMATE PORTRAIT
OF THE PRINCESS OF WALES

ANDREW MORTON

With photographs by Nunn Syndication

MICHAEL O'MARA BOOKS LIMITED

To Lynne, Alexandra and Lydia

First published in Great Britain by
Michael O'Mara Books Ltd, 9 Lion Yard,
11–13 Tremadoc Road, London SW4 7NF

Text copyright © 1990 by Andrew Morton

A CIP catalogue record for this book is available
from the British Library

ISBN 1-85479-077-3

Research by Margaret Holder

Typeset by Florencetype Ltd, Kewstoke, Avon
Printed and bound by Printer Industria Gráfica SA,
Barcelona, Spain

Contents

CHAPTER ONE

Princess in a Gilded Cage

The lilting soprano soared above the hustle and bustle of New Covent Garden Market as the high-spirited young woman serenaded her friends with lively refrains from her favourite musical *My Fair Lady*.

Scurrying porters and barrow boys scarcely noticed the future queen and her entourage as they made their way through the busy market, buying bunches of flowers and a box of fruit early in the morning. Diana played to perfection her part of Eliza Doolittle, the penniless flower girl who was transformed into a Society lady by a kindly professor.

'Lots of chocolates for me to eat, Lots of coal making lots of heat,' sang Diana, word perfect in the lyrics of 'Wouldn't It Be Lovely' from the musical she knows by heart. She even handed out juicy oranges to passers-by as the jolly party made their unrecognized but noisily conspicuous way back home to Kensington.

This innocent, light-hearted foray into the outside world opens a window into that elusive world inhabited by the Princess. She has long identified herself as the royal version of Eliza Doolittle. While she does not come from a humble background – the Spencer family have more aristocratic English blood than the Windsors – she clearly sees the parallels between her own entrance onto the world stage as a gauche, uncertain nineteen-year-old with that of the strong-willed Cockney lass who fought to

The Princess of Wales looks the image of a regal beauty in this revealing study.

retain her own identity within the alien upper class into which she was introduced.

In a similar way Diana has found herself being moulded not only by Prince Charles, thirteen years her senior, but also by a family and courtier class skilled in the subtle arts of smoothly inducing conformity into a system which buttresses the accepted ideals of monarchy.

Her lack of formal education – she gained one O-level in art at grade D – together with her frequent references to being 'as thick as a plank' and having a 'brain the size of a pea' further cement, in Diana's mind, the way her royal progress has matched the Doolittle story. 'She is not dim, just uneducated in the way of so many aristocratic women,' says a former member of her Household. 'But Diana is sharp. Tell her once and she remembers. There is the temptation to adopt the Pygmalion approach and always try and teach her things. Of course, there is so much that she doesn't know but you have to deal with her quite subtly, not talk down to her but approach it at an angle.'

Indeed, the last ten years have been a stern rite of passage. She has had to deal with an inflexible husband struggling to find a purpose in life, the demands of a growing family, the peculiar rigidities of Court life and the obsessive attention of the media which turns a new outfit into front-page news and a moment of levity into a national disaster. As the Duchess of York has discovered to her cost, there is no handbook on how to be royal. It is a process learned by trial and error under the gaze of a critical audience.

'She exudes an inner peace, vitality and poised assurance.'

Indeed it would have been sufficient if Diana had merely coped, enduring the kind of stress that would have sent a lesser spirit reaching for the sleeping pills. As she enters her thirtieth year she exudes an inner peace, vitality and poised assurance which confirm that she has survived and gained strength from a decade which has tested her reserves of endurance and spirit to the limit. 'I haven't seen her laughing so much for ten years,' is how one friend described the Princess following a lively lunchtime get-together. 'She is in good form, she has got it all worked out in herself now.'

Thankfully the days when it was thought the Princess had anorexia nervosa seem to be over. It was perhaps an allusion to her highly strung physical condition that provoked her father, Earl Spencer, to voice his own disquiet. Earl Spencer, once an equerry to King George VI, said, 'In my day the royals only had to do one job a day. My Diana sometimes does two or three. She loves it but I am worried that she is working too hard.'

Those concerns may have been justified in the previous decade when Diana would frequently arrive back at Kensington Palace and literally fall into an armchair, worn out with the nervous exertion of her public engagements. She enters the 1990s with a maturity and experience beyond her years. There is still much to do – she bridles fiercely against the Palace machine – but her sense of purpose is true.

She has reached an affectionate accommodation within her marriage, is at ease with her circle of friends and is clearly delighted with the progress of her sons, Princes William and Harry. *Vogue* photographer Patrick Demarchelier

The Princess is firmly committed to the values of family life expressed publicly in her work for the children's charity Barnardo's *(opposite)* and privately within her much-discussed marriage and the way she is bringing up her children, Princes William and Harry.

'She has a profound dedication to certain values of family life.'

observed this serenity during an afternoon's 'shoot' at Highgrove. He says, 'She seemed to me to be a contented woman. A woman who is satisfied in the company of her children.'

The resolution of her private life – she now feels comfortable with herself and her routine – is reflected in the extra energy she is putting into her public duties. Last year saw a 25 per cent increase in the number of royal engagements she undertook, underlining her growing commitment to her burgeoning portfolio of charities. 'She is enthusiastic about the job, it is one she is tackling with renewed relish,' say friends, sentiments endorsed by her charities. 'The Princess could get away with a hell of a lot less than what she does,' says Roger Singleton, senior director of Barnardo's, the children's charity. 'She goes the extra mile, she has a profound dedication to certain values of family life which finds expression in her work with us.'

It means that, perhaps for the first time, the real character of the Princess is revealed in the pages of her diary. Her social and public round largely reflects the preoccupations of the mature individual rather than the wishes of various courtiers and her husband. Indeed, in this her thirtieth year, she has more command over her destiny than at any time in her royal life.

In Diana's diary the lunches, dinner dates, weddings, christenings, parties, tours, holidays and charity work are entered on the cream parchment in her round, clear handwriting. In fact, the Princess has two diaries. The first, called the Seasons Calendar and embossed with the royal coat of arms, deals with all those engagements which her immediate staff – private secretary Patrick Jephson, her principal lady-in-waiting Anne Beckwith-Smith, and dressers Evelyn Dagley and Fay Appleby – need to know about. Every royal day is divided into three sections – morning, afternoon and evening – while below each calendar date is information about saint's days, known as 'collar days' in royal circles, and the birthdays of other members

The Princess keeps two diaries – an official version for all her public duties and a private diary for her personal life.

of the royal family, including European royals such as King Juan Carlos of Spain and King Michael of Romania. Everything from State visits, banquets, and overseas tours down to visits to her doctor and dentist is entered into the Seasons Calendar. 'Anything which needs preparation by anyone else is included in this diary,' says a member of the Household.

Every morning a small typed card indicating the Princess's engagements for the day is placed on her green-leather-topped desk at Kensington Palace. As she glances over the details she opens her locked desk drawer and pulls out her own diary. The tooled blue leather diary, which is embossed with her own coat of arms, contains

details of those events which she wishes to keep entirely private. This includes dinner parties, family visits and shopping trips.

Her private diary is more than a list of engagements. It contains her thoughts, observations and reminiscences on her royal life. Each member of the royal family keeps a detailed diary and every year they are taken to the Round Tower at Windsor Castle where they are bound and kept for posterity. In a hundred years' time historians will turn the gold-edged pages of Diana's diary and try to imagine the life of the Princess of Wales in the late twentieth century.

The bare announcements in the Court Circular are but the tip of an iceberg of her royal activity. A typical week might involve joining dancers from the English National Ballet in their mews workshop for an hour's workout, an audience in her drawing room at Kensington

Palace with Cardinal Basil Hume, a lunch with her chef Mervyn Wycherley or a private day's session at Relate, the marriage-guidance charity, learning how to counsel a couple whose marriage is in trouble.

Her life is pared down and streamlined so that she can fit as much as possible into her days. On Wednesday mornings, for example, she thinks nothing of slipping through the side entrance of Harrods at 8.30 a.m. to go to the Private Services Suite to try on clothes for casual wear. On one occasion she bought two Yves St Laurent dresses, costing £1,090 ($1,850), in as many minutes before dashing to a nearby Sloane Street shoe store to buy comfortable sandals for a Caribbean holiday on Necker, the private island owned by Richard Branson. Before most people have started work she could have spent £1,200 ($2,040) on holiday wear.

The Princess copes with her fifteen-hour days in a number of ways: it may be a game of tennis, jogging in her white track suit around Kensington Gardens accompanied by her armed detective, a relaxing swim at Buckingham Palace or a strenuous early-morning workout in front of her television set following keep-fit expert Lizzie Webb.

An arduous working day may involve a morning meeting with charity officials to discuss policy, hosting a lunch for High Court judges or Duchy of Cornwall estate managers, opening an Aids unit at a London hospital in the afternoon and attending a film première in the evening. Within this tightly structured life she finds time to take Prince Harry to Wetherby School, help Prince William with his homework and buy gifts for a friend's wedding or a christening.

Little wonder then that a night in front of the television watching a soap opera or a visit with friends to the Odeon cinema on nearby Kensington High Street to see the latest release is bliss.

She relaxes with a circle of friends, most of them married with children, who make up the new royal Court. They organize bridge evenings and dinner parties where the Princess catches up with the latest gossip, is teased about her clothes – she wears slinky outfits after dark – and chuckles at *risqué* jokes. As one pal observes, 'She is a sensitive woman but is also a spunky lady who likes to laugh at sex and finds it far

more amusing if a chap bowls up and talks about the mysteries of the orgasm rather than making awkward conversation about the weather.'

This mischievous side of the Princess is also revealed during all-girls nights out. The evening before her friend Camilla Dunne married Rupert Soames, Diana happily played Tweedle Dee in a mock panto, while her exploits dressed as a policewoman on Prince Andrew's stag night are now notorious. Nightclubs are not her style, much as she enjoys dancing, as ballet star Wayne Sleep discovered when he partnered her on stage at the Royal Opera House for an impromptu performance in front of Prince Charles. 'Whenever I see her she always has that glint in her eye as if to say, "I feel the urge to dance," ' he says.

She enjoys a quieter life at Highgrove, the 353-acre country estate in Gloucestershire, which the Wales have spent a fortune on turning into their weekend retreat. It is an uncomplicated, occasionally eccentric rural lifestyle where their bodyguards frequently double as shepherds and where the family enjoys nude bathing in their outdoor pool. Even though they entertain seldom – the trickle of visitors has included American millionaires Armand Hammer and Walter Annenberg and Prince Hals and Princess Marie Kinsky of Liechtenstein – Diana is an assured and accomplished hostess.

The family leads an unadorned life at Highgrove; 'I want this home to be simple, not like other royal homes,' says Prince Charles emphatically. This austerity can take guests by surprise. At the end of one dinner party where the company enjoyed a main course of Balmoral venison and mushrooms from Windsor, the departing guests were surprised to find the house plunged into darkness as they waited on the forecourt for their cars. Their exhausted royal hosts had gone to bed.

When the Prince and Princess are at Kensington Palace they effectively work as managing directors of separate companies, their lives ruled by their diaries. At Highgrove they can pursue their private interests and plan the future at leisure. That future means their eventual roles as king and queen consort. The corner of the Highgrove rose garden gives a clue, albeit cryptic, that that day may be fast approaching.

Sunshine and surf are not normally associated with the royal family's winter holiday. They prefer the chilly pleasures of the Queen's windswept Sandringham estate in Norfolk. But the Princess, who feels at home in the playgrounds of the rich, has broken with tradition and taken several winter breaks on the island of Necker, the Caribbean hideaway owned by millionaire Richard Branson. She was joined by her mother Frances Shand-Kydd and her sister Jane Fellowes, together with their children and assorted nannies and bodyguards.

Charles is planning to turn his home-grown rose petals into the Holy Oil for use in his anointing as monarch. Is this an imaginative indulgence or is there a plan, known only within the immediate family, for the Queen to abdicate her throne in favour of her eldest son?

Their eventual destiny gives the royal couple considerable thought about their own relationship. It is probably the most discussed marriage in the world and possibly the least understood. It is a partnership where, whatever their mutual difficulties, divorce is not an option. The *My Fair Lady* analogy of the young flower girl who was moulded by Professor Higgins, learned her part in society and went her own way, is one which has served Diana well.

She was the sacrificial virgin bride, in love with the romantic idea of being a Princess and slavishly devoted to a man with considerable charm but with a life already fulfilled by the essentially masculine pursuits of hunting, shooting and fishing. Marriage was an inevitable duty, his choice of bride engineered by the machinations of the grandmother he reveres and Diana's grandmother, the Queen Mother's lady-in-waiting, Ruth, Lady Fermoy.

In the early years of their married life Prince Charles was a very tactile husband – as when he publicly squeezed Diana's backside at polo.

In the early days the Prince guided his adoring but strong-willed wife while maintaining his bachelor habits. It was an awkward transition – 'slight communications problems' as the royal family euphemistically termed the stormy clashes of wills between Diana and Charles. Quarrels were inevitable between a man of inflexible routine used to being the centre of attention and a young woman insecure of her position and jealous of potential rivals. 'It was like working for two rival pop stars,' recalls one former member of staff.

'The cheerful ring of laughter was replaced by a scratchy silence when Diana would ignore staff and their courtesies.'

Their arguments flared so frequently and abruptly that at one point Michael Shea, the Queen's former Press Secretary, would instruct visitors to Kensington Palace to ignore the couple if an argument developed. The tension and continual strain of her royal life caused Diana to shed too much weight and teeter on the edge of anorexia nervosa, the slimmers' disease. Prince Charles was so concerned that he read Sheila MacLeod's book on the subject while Lily Snipp, Diana's dancing teacher, recorded in her diaries that her doctor, Michael Linnett, advised the Princess to try and increase her weight.

Perhaps the happiest days followed the birth of Prince Harry. It was helped by an easier pregnancy than her first combined with her growing acceptance of her royal role. The Wales' homes at Kensington Palace and Highgrove rang with the sound of shared laughter. Gradually, almost imperceptibly, the laughter died and a chill set in which affected everyone touched by it. The cheerful ring of laughter was replaced by a scratchy silence when Diana would ignore her staff and their courtesies. 'You just never knew where you were with her,' says one member of staff. 'When there was a chill on, you always thought it was your fault.'

When they were first married, Prince Charles and Princess Diana went everywhere together as the Prince taught his wife the royal routine. Now they have separate timetables, different daily schedules and separate circles of friends, which inevitably leads to speculation about their lives.

On her regular walks around the estate at Highgrove she deliberately took avoiding action if she saw a member of staff on the horizon. She ordered the back stairs, which had been boarded up since the 1960s when Harold Macmillan's son, Maurice, owned the house, to be restored so that she saw as little as possible of her employees. Her dissatisfaction and rebellion against her position was translated into hostility towards the people who served her. Everyone suffered. Some members of staff lost weight, others could not sleep, and Ken Stronach, Charles' devoted valet, was sent to a Harley Street specialist when he complained of chest palpitations and blinding headaches. The diagnosis was that he was suffering from stress caused by his work. When this was reported to the Prince he said tetchily, 'Well, that's what happens when you work for me.'

The silences were not helped by the growing media interest in the royal marriage. Speculation reached fever pitch in 1987 when Prince Charles stayed at Balmoral for thirty-three consecutive days while the Princess remained in London with the children. The rumours, fuelled by lurid stories which had trickled out from the early days of their marriage, created a climate where American fashion houses were drawing up million-dollar contracts for Diana's new career as a model when her divorce was finalized.

The Princess made a stalwart defence of her marriage difficulties during one animated cocktail-party conversation. 'I know what people are thinking but inevitably we are going to be frequently apart, it's the nature of the job,' she argued. 'Our marriage is very good but we don't see as much of each other as we should.' Then, in a startling send-up of the endless speculation, she continued, 'Anyway, why shouldn't I take a black, Catholic lover? Or at any rate a black lover?'

Naturally the hysteria hurt. 'It didn't help them reconcile their differences,' notes a friend diplomatically. The reality of living with the Prince rather than adoring from afar, the permanent loss of freedom and the influence of a boisterous Duchess of York cast a long shadow over the fairy tale.

For a time the effervescent Duchess of York was a strong influence in the life of the Princess.

'Prince Charles is the elder brother Diana never had.'

During this difficult period there were few rows, only endless simmering silences which remorselessly wore down their staff. Indeed the only public row between the couple occurred when he unexpectedly brought a party of polo friends to Highgrove one summer's afternoon. While there was a sharp exchange of words this is hardly out of the ordinary in any marriage.

Since the difficulties of the late 1980s the royal couple have reached a friendly alliance. Maybe it was the trauma of the Klosters avalanche which so nearly claimed his life, the growing distance between Diana and Fergie, her one-time close companion, or simply the inevitable compromises that have to be made to make life tolerable, which have helped forge an amicable union. While they now lead essentially separate lives with different friends and contrasting interests, she is endlessly supportive of Charles, fiercely protecting him from the merest hint of criticism, however well meant. She is still fond of him even though the grand passion has gone. 'He is really the elder brother she never had,' observes a friend. 'Before she married she didn't really know what she was letting herself in for. It was all rather forced on her by her grandmother and the Queen Mother. Now she knows where she stands and she is ticking along very nicely thank you.'

While they occasionally share the marital bed, more frequently they sleep apart, Diana in the six-foot wide Georgian four poster, Charles next door in a single sofa bed. The silk cushion on her bed bearing the motif 'You have to kiss a lot of frogs to find a Prince' is a poignant reminder of days when the fairy tale and romantic reality were the same. 'I don't envy them, I just pity them their fate,' says one former member of staff. After ten years of marriage, friendship has replaced infatuation, understanding companionship has supplanted mutual indifference – much to the relief of their friends and staff. It is a marital *status quo* that will serve the couple well for the foreseeable future.

Gallant as always, Prince Charles kisses his wife's hand as he collects a trophy after a match at the Guards' Polo Club at Smith's Lawn, Windsor.

Mutual support and old-fashioned gallantry are still writ large in their lives such as when Prince Charles visited Park House, Diana's birthplace at Sandringham, in the early 1980s. During his tour of the building he discovered his wife's signature on a window frame along with scores of other names and telephone numbers. The white-framed window had been used over the years as a family notepad. In a romantic gesture the man described by friends as a 'charming male chauvinist' had the entire frosted glass window transferred to Highgrove as a lasting reminder of Diana's childhood.

Meanwhile, the Princess marked their seventh wedding anniversary by contacting Gilly Lynne, the choreographer of *Phantom of the Opera*, hiring a film crew and making a video of herself dancing and singing her favourite song from the show, 'All I Ask of You'.

The underlying romantic rapport shared by the couple was displayed when Diana performed an impromptu shimmy in front of Charles during a banquet in the magnificent setting of Chambord Château in the Loire Valley in France. They had just watched a performance of semi-nude fan dancing by Zizi Jeanmaire, who, at sixty-three, is the 'Queen Mother' of cabaret. Her age and the incongruity of this sort of show in such elegant surroundings delighted the Princess and inspired her own pastiche.

These days the couple make a professional team, sharing the burdens of public life and bolstering one another. On joint visits or foreign tours a glance, a gesture or a crisp phrase is their shorthand of emotional sustenance. During their triumphant visit to Paris they stood

For once the strain showed when the Prince and Princess shook hands with 160 dignitaries before a banquet at the Elysée Palace in Paris.

with fixed smiles and glazed expressions at the Elysée Palace as they greeted a line-up of 160 guests. Diana sighed, 'At last it's over,' while Charles nodded and replied, 'What a job!'

Psychologist Anne Cook cast a cool professional eye over this interplay when she joined them for lunch during their visit to Melbourne in Australia. She recalls, 'Her eyes are never far from his. They seem to know what each other is doing and thinking without a lot of verbal communication. A brief look is sufficient. That suggests that their marriage is based on trust.'

The Princess made clear the depth of her faith and support when she dined with Armand Hammer, the oil magnate and philanthropist. They were talking about Charles. Hammer recalls saying to Diana, 'You know, I can't say "no" to him, whatever he asks me to do. I have so much confidence in him that if he asked me to jump through that window there, I think I'd jump through the window.' She smiled and replied, 'Well, I'd jump right after you.'

Just as the subtle development of her marriage will be made clear to historians as they turn the pages of Diana's diary so the differences due to the fact that Diana has lived an ordinary life, while Charles has been constricted from birth to the open prison of royalty, will become apparent. Diana has cleaned floors for £1 ($1.70) an hour, served canapés at cocktail parties and acted as nanny for well-heeled friends. By normal standards she has enjoyed a privileged lifestyle and yet she has still queued at supermarket checkouts and fumed in London traffic jams. By contrast, Prince Charles has been institutionalized within the royal cocoon, aware of how the rest of the world lives but never truly understanding the pressures and frustrations.

For all their wealth and privileges Charles and Diana live in an open prison. It is a world where anything impulsive is impossible. Every moment of the day Diana is shadowed. As a professional, she accepts the presence of photographers at a royal engagement but what she finds harder to bear is the perpetual presence of the security both inside and outside her homes. At times it

can feel very claustrophobic. At Kensington Palace and Highgrove spy cameras watch her every move. When she goes for a walk in the fields surrounding Highgrove the unblinking eye of a camera swivels and tracks her while the two policemen who constantly patrol the grounds discreetly alter their perambulations so that they have her constantly in their sight. In the police post she is watched on one of nine television monitors. At night a policeman patrols the house while an armed detective sleeps on the floor above hers. It is little wonder then that Diana feels a helpless frustration at her caged existence. She says resentfully, 'I would love to lock all the police in the Highgrove lodge and throw away the key.'

Wherever she travels, the Princess is serenaded by the 'Nikon choir' – the cameramen who capture her every move. She has now overcome her nerves and here, at the Cannes Film Festival, displays quizzical amusement at the jostling photographers.

'For all their wealth and privileges Charles and Diana live in an open prison.'

It explains why she occasionally makes late-night 'escape bids' on her own so that she can see close friends like her former flatmate Carolyn Bartholomew or her lady-in-waiting, Anne Beckwith-Smith, when she joins her for a snack of scrambled eggs, a chat and a couple of hours watching television.

Late one evening, acting on a whim, she left her Kensington Palace apartment and drove to a friend's central London flat, picking up a girl-friend on the way. When the young man answered the frantic midnight knock on the door he was disconcerted to see a mutual friend and the Princess, a towelling dressing gown over her nightie. They chatted over coffee until the early hours and then Diana went happily off into the night, like a naughty sixth-former who has made a successful foray from her boarding school after lights out.

Charles handles the constraints of his position differently. Cares of the outside world are entirely alien. When he once announced, 'Diana only married me so that she could go through red traffic lights,' he was speaking more truthfully than he realized, not about her life but about his. The Prince is a stranger to reality, his priorities anchored, not in the facts of everyday life, but in a highly structured and artificial royal world where he is waited on hand and foot.

On one occasion when Charles was complaining about having to plan his life six months in advance, the Cockney photographer Arthur Edwards retorted, 'I don't know what you have to worry about, Sir, you don't even have to pack your wallet in the morning.' There was more than a nugget of truth in that riposte – the Prince's valet, Ken Stronach, does that for him, ensuring that any money he carries is new or at least steamed and pressed with a hot iron. Any minor alteration in his obdurate routine becomes a major issue. One valet was driven to distraction when he mislaid the Prince's fountain pen. 'Where's my pen? Where's my pen?' he repeated endlessly, refusing to allow the subject to drop for days. His valet left shortly afterwards.

It is here that Diana is the soothing emollient. She is sensitive to the Prince's moods, understands the frustrations of his position, and acts as a buffer between him and his staff when things go wrong. While Diana simply shrugs her shoulders and tries to adapt when problems emerge, Charles tends to become tetchy. She is usually able to jolly him out of his irritation and make him laugh. During a visit to a smelting works in Victoria, south Australia, she saw the funny side when her protective white hat was too big and came down to her eyebrows. Charles's thoughts concerned the administrative blunder. Again, on a trip to Oman he demanded that a photograph of himself and the Princess be changed because the picture had been reversed and showed his military orders the wrong way round. Diana passed it off as 'one of those things'.

The television personality Jimmy Savile shares Diana's ability to make the Prince see the absurdity of his regal expectations. Savile, who plays the part of Court Jester to the Establishment with consummate skill, is a regular visitor to Kensington and Buckingham Palaces, as well as the Prime Minister's country residence of Chequers. As the unofficial clown he articulates opinions which courtiers can only think. On one occasion Charles was fretting because his royal train was a couple of minutes late. There was nothing anyone could do but the Prince became increasingly fussed by the delay. 'What do you want me to do? Shoot the stationmaster?' asked Savile in mock seriousness. 'All right, I'll shoot the stationmaster.' His intervention dissipated the tension.

By contrast, the Princess finds that the nonsense of so much of the convoluted courtesy inherent in royal life only serves to tickle her sense of the ridiculous. When Les Rudd, chief executive of Turning Point, was proudly showing Diana around a project in Worksop, Nottinghamshire, he opened what he assumed was a door leading to another part of the building. He discovered to his horror that it was the broom cupboard and all the brushes cascaded to her feet. 'She still teases me about it,' he says ruefully.

It was Charles who was the butt of her mirth when they met the high-kicking chorus girls from the Moulin Rouge nightclub in Paris. As they went along the line-up the Prince launched into his finest French. 'Bonsoir, mademoiselle,' intoned the Prince to one young woman, resplendent in her feathers and finery. 'I had better stop you there, I'm from Bexhill-on-Sea,' came the reply. While Charles was momentarily nonplussed, Diana collapsed in gales of laughter.

A sense of humour as well as organizational ability are vital qualities for a modern Princess. It is as well that Diana has a tidy mind. Twice a year the royal couple and their two Households meet around the dining table at Kensington Palace to sift the shoal of requests for visits from local councils, hospitals, industry and the hundred or so organizations they are closely associated with.

Not only does the Princess have to juggle her life around her husband's schedule, she also has the needs of her sons to consider. Their school holidays, carol concerts, sports days and outings are entered into Diana's diary first, her other engagements clustering around the timetables of Ludgrove and Wetherby schools which Prince William and Prince Harry now attend. She thoroughly enjoys these outings and her delight was unconfined when she won the mothers' race at a school sports day. 'This is the first time in my life I've ever won anything like this,' she said.

A ready sense of humour has served Diana well in her royal life. When things go wrong on tour, Charles is liable to be annoyed while Diana sees the funny side of the situation.

Her arms pumping vigorously, the Princess wins the Mothers' Race at her son's school sports day. She was genuinely delighted by her achievement – 'This is the first time in my life I've ever won anything like this,' she said. Her victory did not prevent her enjoying a game of 'bulls and matadors' with Prince Harry and his friends afterwards.

'The Princess enjoys regular consultations with a well-established but discreet Society astrologer.'

Wherever possible she ensures that working lunches do not overrun so that she can collect Prince Harry from school. Indeed, she chose to send Prince William to Ludgrove preparatory school as a weekly boarder so that he can spend the weekends with his family at Highgrove. Traditionally, the education of the heir to the throne exercises the minds of the Sovereign, the Prime Minister and the Archbishop of Canterbury as well as the parents themselves. It has been suggested in Court circles that the Princess resisted the arguments of the Duke of Edinburgh to send William to Gordonstoun in Scotland because eventually she wants him to attend Eton, the public school where her brother Viscount Althorp and many of her friends were educated.

However, Diana has an extra incentive to vet the future progress of her eldest son. The Princess, who takes an active interest in astrology, is acutely aware of the destiny mapped out for her husband, herself and her sons. Born under the sign of Cancer, she knows that numerous astrologers have predicted Prince Charles will never become king, that she will be denied the title of queen consort and is destined to re-marry.

The prophecies of the modern-day soothsayers also indicate that Prince William is likely to become king after a constitutional crisis, with the Duke and Duchess of York acting as regents. While she is aware of the predictions she is not daunted by them. Unlike Nancy Reagan, who altered the routine of the American President if the stars were unfavourable, Diana's interest stems from a mother's natural curiosity about the fate of her family. This interest manifests itself in the regular consultations the Princess enjoys with a Society astrologer. It is something of a royal fad. Her next-door neighbour, Princess Michael of Kent, a Capricorn, has frequent visits from her own star-gazer.

During her forty-minute sessions Diana will have been told that her stars indicate a third child in September 1991 and that the early years of the decade are a propitious period to try and improve her marriage.

Certainly William would scorn his mother's concerns. He is developing into a robust, determined and self-confident boy. Once it was finally decided to send him to Ludgrove, the eight-year-old schoolboy took it upon himself to telephone San Lorenzo's, Diana's favourite restaurant, and book a table for two as a surprise celebration. 'I would not have had the self-confidence to do that at eighteen let alone eight,' remarks one family friend.

When staff leave royal employment it is William who more likely than not will make the farewell speech of thanks. His words are measured, controlled and, in true Windsor fashion, he stands with his hands behind his back like his grandfather, the Duke of Edinburgh. Those who see the Wales regularly *en famille* regard William as the strongest of the foursome. He is the one person who will stand eye to eye with his father and shout, 'I can't' or 'I won't' with regal defiance. It is little wonder that Charles, used to sycophants and 'yes' men, finds it hard to cope with such a strong-willed little boy. 'When he gives you that searing Spencer stare he can be quite intimidating,' says a member of staff.

Yet beneath his tough exterior – Diana wryly describes him as 'my little thug' – William is a generous, spirited boy who adores his parents and his younger brother, Prince Harry, while doting on his various nannies. When the royal couple visited the Middle East he smuggled a note into his mother's luggage which said, 'Dear Mummy and Papa, Have a lovely time in the Middle East but hurry home soon because I will miss you.'

By contrast Prince Harry is a much less imposing character. 'Laid back' is the description most often used by those who have observed him. His birth, after an easy pregnancy, gave Charles and Diana much joy, leading to a renaissance in their relationship. Like many second children, he learned to speak much later than his elder brother, which is hardly surprising given William's talkative nature. Harry's outstanding quality is that he exudes a serenity, an inner glow, remarkable in one so young. Perhaps his

peaceful personality is best expressed when he is on horseback. Whereas William is like his father in that he is only a competent if enthusiastic rider, Harry has an instinctive rapport with horses – rather like his aunt, Princess Anne. When he first sat astride Smokey, his Shetland pony, he looked so natural it was as if he had been born in the saddle.

Diana tries to bring out the best in her boys and understand their different natures. As Carolyn Bartholomew, her close friend, observes, 'They're terrific boys and Diana's a great mother. She's very responsible and responsive to their individual natures and aware of all their character differences. Both Charles and Diana are proud of William's self-confidence and independence and are equally appreciative of Harry's thoughtfulness and gentle nature.'

As she balances the needs of her family and the wishes of the nation she inevitably errs on the side of her loved ones. 'There's no doubt what comes first with the Princess,' says a Palace official. 'First it's her children and her husband, and then her official role.'

This is true for much of the time. However, there is one person whose wishes take precedence over every other diary date in Diana's busy life – the Queen. Courtiers use the terse acronym 'MOTG' to describe the Sovereign's requests. It means 'Morally Obliged To Go' which essentially summarizes the Queen's authority over the Princess and other members of the royal family. She does not lay down the law as some would have us believe. Her requests are courteously made through the discreet network of private secretaries. A call from the Queen's private secretary Sir Robert Fellowes to Diana's private secretary Patrick Jephson would be on the lines of, 'The Queen would think it marvellous if the Princess of Wales could possibly join her at such and such an event.' The royal equivalent of a parliamentary three-line whip is a sentence which begins, 'The Queen would

Above: **Prince William has developed into a supremely confident schoolboy with a strong streak of Spencer sternness running through his character.**

Below: **Like any other boy, Prince Harry is oblivious to the rest of the world as he enjoys an ice-cream during a holiday in the Isles of Scilly.**

'There are few more miserable occasions in Diana's diary than when the Queen invites her horseriding.'

appreciate the attendance of the Princess of Wales . . .'

These invitations are usually for the major events of the royal season – the State Opening of Parliament, Ascot, Trooping the Colour, or a visit by an overseas Head of State, or the Remembrance Day ceremony at the Cenotaph. There is never any question of declining the invitation however pressing other engagements may be.

Diana's respect for the institution of monarchy is absolute. As one courtier remarks, 'She is very serious about the Crown. After all she was brought up in an aristocratic family who regard the monarchy as the pinnacle of the social hierarchy.' Generations of Spencers have provided indispensable service to the Crown. Her father Earl Spencer was equerry to King George VI while her other ancestors have held Court posts as diverse as Lord Lieutenant, Groom of the Stole and Privy Seal. So when the Queen issues an invitation, Princess Diana notes the date in her diary with alacrity.

While her deference to the throne is total, Diana's relationship with the holder of the office is essentially formal. Like every other royal lady apart from the Queen Mother, Diana drops a full Court curtsy to the Queen, kissing her on the left and right cheeks and finally her hand. Thereafter the Princess addresses her mother-in-law as 'Ma'am' and not the cosier 'Lillibet' used by the Queen's blood relatives.

The Princess often makes light of these rather stiff encounters by joking that it is like standing on a moving carpet because the Queen is surrounded by so many yapping corgis. However, there is no disguising the lack of personal rapport. The Queen has rarely, if ever, visited the Prin-

Opposite: **However full Diana's diary may be, she never refuses an invitation from the Queen to attend the major events of the royal year such as the Remembrance Day ceremony at the Cenotaph.**

cess at Kensington Palace and she has only made one fleeting visit to Highgrove. This was shortly after the birth of Prince Harry. She landed on the lawns in a red Wessex helicopter of the Queen's Flight, made her way to the second-floor nursery to see her fourth grandchild and then departed fifteen minutes later.

It is not surprising that the Sovereign and the future Queen Consort have few points of reference. The Queen's priorities are, in the words of her staff, 'dogs, horses, people'. If she had her way she would live in the country and breed animals. Diana, who is a metropolitan person at heart, tells her friends, 'In another incarnation the last thing I would ever want to be is a horse.' Indeed, there are few more miserable occasions in Diana's diary than when the Queen invites her for a gentle ride along the lanes around Sandringham House. The Princess always looks the very picture of nervous reluctance. Her timidity is understandable. As a child she broke her arm when she was thrown from her horse. She says, 'I cannot stand riding. It terrifies me. Just the thought of getting on a horse fills me with fear.' During her royal career she has attempted to overcome her fears but without success.

This reluctance extends to the country pursuits of hunting, shooting and fishing which the Windsors so enjoy. Shrewd charity organizers and friends invite her to events in August and September so that she has a perfect excuse to escape the suffocating boredom of Balmoral. During Queen Victoria's reign every member of the royal family had to make the annual summer

The Queen's love of horses and dogs is not shared by Diana who broke her arm in a fall.

pilgrimage to the monarch's Highland retreat. These days it is more flexible, much to Diana's relief.

Although she is at heart a traditionalist, Diana harbours a streak of the non-conformist in her heart, a trait she no doubt inherited from her mother, Frances, who shocked Society when she left Earl Spencer and ran off with a wallpaper company executive. Her schoolfriend Sophie Lane, who joined Diana on several holidays when they were teenagers, noted this characteristic: 'At school she was a rebel in a quiet sort of way. She saw school as something to be endured. In those days she was rather anti-Establishment. She wouldn't co-operate with things.'

In the royal world this faint rebellion is seen in her refusal to wear gloves and stockings – the required accessories of Court formality. She uses her fashions as the mute language to subtly show her distance from the prevailing order. A white suit she wore for the passing-out parade at the Royal Military Academy, Sandhurst, was a witty parody of a military uniform, while her Mary Queen of Scots gown and outsize cross, worn on one evening engagement, was seen in some quarters as exhibiting her distance from the Protestant family she now represents. Richard Blackwell, Hollywood dressmaker and author of the famous 'Ten Worst Dressed Women' list, was right when he noted, 'Diana has rebelled

Diana is a traditionalist with a gently rebellious streak in her character which is publicly expressed in her clothes. However, her 'drum majorette' outfit worn for the passing-out parade at Sandhurst did not win the approval of senior officers.

While the Princess enjoys a purely formal and respectful relationship with the Queen, she is deeply loyal to the institution of the monarchy.

and become the marvellously fashionable young girl she should be, instead of the copy of an old lady the Queen tried to make of her when she married Charles.'

This reluctance to conform to Court protocol and procedure is shown in her inability to speak French fluently. As French is the official Court language, used in diplomatic circles and in conversation with foreign royal families, this is a distinct disadvantage. Every other member of the royal family, including the Duchess of York, can converse easily in French, and several royals, the Duke of Edinburgh and Prince and Princess Michael of Kent in particular, are well versed in German.

The Princess's visit to the fashionable Champneys health farm when the Court was at Sandringham and her holidays in Majorca as the guest of King Juan Carlos of Spain, when the Queen is in Balmoral, are further signs of her faintly defiant nature. Indeed how many royals make regular record requests on commercial pop radio? Diana does, calling herself 'Disco Di from Kensington' when she calls disc jockey Graham Dene on London's Capital Radio. She is such a fan that she even telephones him on his birthday.

Indeed, the more she observes the rigidities of the British Court, the more she contrasts it with the easy dignity and affable approachability of King Juan Carlos of Spain and his Court. If the monarchy is to change – and she is not an unwilling reformer – she would like to see it modelled along the Spanish lines. It is a popular institution but without the unhealthy hysteria which surrounds the British royal family. Respect from outside is matched by a relaxed atmosphere within.

In tandem with her reflections on the nature of the monarchy is a growing distrust of the courtier class who advise on the public engagements for her diary. It is a suspicion she shares with Prince Charles. As he says wearily, 'We don't run our staff, they run us.' The Household, made up of aristocrats, diplomats, military officers and the occasional well-bred businessman,

The Princess admires the Spanish monarchy for its relaxed style, but certain formalities still have to be observed. Unfortunately, tight skirts do not make for an elegant curtsy, as the Princess demonstrated when she met King Juan Carlos and Queen Sophia of Spain in Majorca.

advise and organize the royal family, interpreting their wishes and toning down their wilder excesses. This subtle interaction between the personal and public life of the royal family has changed little since Tudor times. 'The only difference from the days of Henry VIII is that we don't get our heads chopped off,' remarks one former member of the Household drily.

A successful courtier is a cross between a psychologist and politician, discreetly able to trim the sails of counsel depending which way the royal wind is blowing. It means that those who advise the Prince and Princess can be headed off course depending on the prevailing royal mood. Diana's notorious early-morning chills can becalm the best-laid plans.

Those who disagree too frequently with Diana or Charles eventually find themselves in the cold – as many advisors have discovered to their cost. 'There is a magic line that courtiers can cross once or twice. Cross it too often and you are out,' says one former courtier. 'That is not a stable basis for a career.'

Within the Wales' Household the rivalry between Charles and Diana means that a courtier is on one side or the other. There is no middle course. It is a system which favours 'yes' men, a fact that Charles recognizes even though his autocratic behaviour perpetuates it. He distrusts all advisors, fearing that they are conspiring to steer him away from the real world. During one royal tour a Foreign Office diplomat put forward a cogent argument for a certain course of action. Charles demurred, saying, 'But you are the Establishment.' His response left the official wondering what position the Prince saw himself occupying.

The Prince's judgment of people is quite arbitrary. 'An intellectual pillow bearing the impression of the last person who spoke to him,' was one unkind though not untypical description of the Prince. In the television documentary on the lives of the Prince and Princess he was advised by courtiers to leave the references to his conversations with his plants on the cutting-room floor. He refused, citing various letters from the public in his support and giving their views more weight than his advisors'. The result was that he became the butt of cartoonists and caricaturists for months afterwards.

By contrast Diana has the immeasurable advantage that she can make her own decisions with reference to the outside world – a modest accomplishment but a vital requirement in the mirrored universe of royalty. Unlike Charles, she has maintained a reasonably stable staff. She is a woman of many moods and while she can be difficult and temperamental she is also a kind and thoughtful boss. Examples of her considerate nature abound. She made a special hospital visit to see Maria Burrell, the wife of her butler at Highgrove, when she had her first baby, befriended Sarah Lindsay, the wife of Hugh Lindsay who was tragically killed in the Klosters avalanche, and was a tower of strength to her dresser, Fay Appleby, when she suffered from cancer.

Thoughtfulness is one thing but experience in Palace politics is quite another. The replacement this year of her private secretary – her

long-serving lady-in-waiting Anne Beckwith-Smith – by a naval officer was viewed with alarm by several more progressive courtiers. They saw it as Diana being out-manoeuvred by those who dominate the Old Guard at the Palace. For such a sensitive post, where female intuition and tact are prerequisites, it was argued that a woman rather than a military man would be more appropriate.

It is perhaps for this reason that Diana is increasingly turning to a tightly knit circle of friends as an informal secretariat to give advice and opinions. In the early days of her royal career, many of her friends disappeared from her life. Now that she is in control of her royal life, their names are beginning to reappear more frequently in the pages of her diary.

> **'In a decade she has built up a wardrobe worth over £1.2 million ($2.04 million) to become the most celebrated princess of the century.'**

The Princess is a different woman from the royal Eliza Doolittle of her early twenties. She is now mistress of two houses, in charge of more than twenty staff and thinks little of spending £200,000 ($340,000) a year on her health, beauty and fashions. The days when she spent four hours rummaging through the wardrobes of her flatmates before she mixed and matched a suitable outfit for a date with Prince Charles are gone for good. By 1991 she will have built up a wardrobe worth over £1.2 million ($2.04 million) to become perhaps the most celebrated princess of the century. As historian Sir Roy Strong says, 'The Princess is investing in a new look and is wearing jewellery with panache and daring. The nearest royal comparison is with Queen Alexandra who was both beautiful and good. Diana is the name for the future.'

The sophistication of her grooming – she has now pared down her designers to Catherine Walker, Victor Edelstein and a handful of others – symbolizes the way she has thought through her life so that what she wears reflects her real character. Yet the surface glamour revealed in

The Princess's use of jewellery is as imaginative as it is striking. She is not afraid of wearing fakes or altering family heirlooms.

the pages of her diary has not changed the kindly soul underneath. Recently she found time in her schedule to organize a surprise dinner party to cheer up her former flatmate Carolyn Bartholomew whose dog had died. She is generous too in her choice of gifts for her friends and relations – not a trait normally associated with the royal family. In an average year she spends about £40,000 ($68,000) on presents and charitable donations.

One close friend observes, 'She really is the most caring lady I know. It really does come from the heart.' Understandably this view is shared by her father Earl Spencer who says, 'She has a natural dignity, she knows how to behave, how to treat people. She can see different points of view. It's something quite natural to her. The qualities are just there, they are hereditary.'

It is that quality of compassion which has enabled her to take on a portfolio of charity work in causes allied to society's greatest problems. Her work for Aids, leprosy, drug and alcohol abuse have earned her international respect. This work has a high price in emotional commitment and there are times when sympathy turns to tears. Perhaps one of the saddest moments of her royal year was when she learned of the death of a courageous teenage girl whom she met at an awards ceremony. Roger Singleton of Barnardo's broke the news to her and recalls, 'It made a real emotional impact on her. It illustrates this blend of personal concern and professionalism which is the hallmark of her work for charities. There is nothing superficial about her response, there is a warmth about the Princess, a charisma almost.'

Diana faced her most severe test in New York, a city which takes a perverse pride in ignoring the rich and famous when they visit. But her tours of a children's Aids centre in Harlem and a hostel for the homeless proved that she was a lot more than an attractive blonde in a ballgown.

Diplomat Francis Cornish was assistant private secretary to Prince Charles in the early 1980s and helped guide the Princess during the first few months of her royal career. By coincidence Cornish, now attached to the British Embassy in Washington, was one of the moving forces behind Diana's triumphant visit. He says, 'New Yorkers expected her to go to Tiffany's and

Diana faced one of the sternest tests of her royal career when she visited New York. However, her friendly self-assurance disarmed her critics in a city which takes a positive pleasure in ignoring the rich and famous.

Fifth Avenue black-tie dinners so they were considerably impressed that the Princess decided to do it her way. I was very impressed in the way she conducted herself in New York. She was not putting on an act, it was not a performance. Her behaviour was genuine and very effective. All the signs were there from the early days and she proved she could do it.'

The Eliza Doolittle Princess has come of age and the pages of Diana's diary bear silent witness to the royal transformation.

CHAPTER TWO

At the Court of Princess Diana

The waiters in the Chinese restaurant in central London adopt a look of bored world-weariness. 'We have some prince or other coming,' says the *maître d'* of Mr Wings, with a scarcely disguised shrug of uninterest. His indifference is understandable. This corner of Old Brompton Road and Earl's Court sees probably more deposed princes, Arab sheiks and counts drive by in their Mercedes than any part of London outside Belgravia. It boasts a certain notoriety as a royal landmark. Just along the road is the flat once owned by the American actress Katherine Stark, better known as Koo, a former girlfriend of Prince Andrew, who was subject to the daily attentions of the international paparazzi. Also around the corner is red-bricked Coleherne Court, the bachelor apartment owned by Lady Diana Spencer.

So there is surprise bordering on panic when, a little late, the Princess of Wales walks through the door to make a brief return to her old stomping ground. The restaurant is so full of low-hanging shrubbery that Diana, 5 feet 10 inches in her stockinged feet, has to duck her head as she makes her way to the table.

At lunchtime Mr Wings is quiet and the intimate alcoves make it the perfect place for a discreet meeting. However, Diana's two Scotland Yard bodyguards take no chances. As the table was booked by a friend and the restaurant is not a regular royal haunt they have

The Court of the Princess of Wales is a combination of formality and friendship.

looked the place over the night before, spoken briefly to the manager and moved the chosen table further away from prying eyes. Even though it is an informal lunch, a gathering of friends who have known one another for half a lifetime, nothing is left to chance. Anything touched by royalty generates people, protocol and paperwork – even a day which the Princess chooses to spend privately.

At the start of a typical week a white typed sheet of Kensington Palace notepaper is handed to staff informing them of Diana's business. For this particular luncheon her dresser Evelyn Dagley – Diana calls her Ev – will have laid out the smart but inconspicuous two-piece suit, court shoes and jewellery while more staff, knowing their services will not be required at lunchtime, busy themselves with other duties.

However, as soon as Diana slips behind the steering wheel of her blue Jaguar XJS and drives from the south entrance at Kensington Palace, another sphere of service starts to spin into action. At Scotland Yard her whereabouts are monitored by computer. Royal bodyguards use their high-frequency radios sparingly – there is little need as route changes are rare. In a quiet side street near the restaurant an ambulance waits in readiness. Not that anyone doubts the chef's abilities. This is merely standard procedure. The London Ambulance Service is informed of every royal movement so that even when Diana goes shopping there is an ambulance on alert. A similar policy is adopted by the fire brigade. Every time the Princess flies over

'Every minute, every hour in Diana's life involves a platoon of people.'

London in a bright red Wessex helicopter of the Queen's Flight a fire brigade officer goes to the roof of the headquarters building by the River Thames and watches her progress through binoculars, relaying the helicopter's movements to the control room.

Every minute, every hour, every day in the life of the Princess of Wales involves a platoon of people. Some have become her friends, others remain firmly in the background. On or off duty, the Court of Princess Diana is a hive of activity.

Unfortunately, no one has told the chef that he is cooking for the Princess of Wales. 'It is Diana, it is Diana,' is the strangled cry from the excited waiters who tumble into the tiled basement demanding dishes immediately. Galvanized into action, he wipes his hands on his striped apron, adjusts his white cap, and feverishly starts work.

As she takes her seat Diana is calm at the centre of the activity which inevitably follows her every movement. Today she is enjoying a day off and so perhaps no more than twenty people are swept up in the royal whirl. She is all kisses and smiles as the two men friends, both Old Etonians, make brief neckbows and the ladies drop neat effortless half curtsies. While protocol requires deference, her friends perform these obeisances out of respect. The rest of the world may know her as Her Royal Highness the Princess of Wales but they call her Diana and are immensely proud of her, all the more so because they understand the complexities of moving into the world of the Windsors.

As with any gathering of friends, the conversation concerns mutual pals, careers, and children. Diana confides that she is anxious about her choice of Ludgrove preparatory school for Prince William. However, she is soon reassured by her friends, who know numerous old boys who speak well of the £6,300 ($10,700) a year Berkshire school.

Diana has always been a good listener, a positive advantage now that listening is as much

The Princess sports a sweater with the symbol of the London Underground, an appropriate emblem for a woman who loves the metropolis.

a part of her job description as wearing a tiara. Her technique is deceptively simple – looking directly into the eyes of whoever is speaking. Indeed her clear blue eyes are the first feature most people notice and she has mesmerized many powerful men from the former Canadian Premier Pierre Trudeau to the Australian Prime Minister Bob Hawke. Her twinkling eyes quickly betray her other striking quality – her ready smile and easy laughter. She cocks her head to one side, chin on hand, her face ever ready to adopt a pose of sympathy or shared humour.

This lunchtime there is much to amuse her as the waiters bring dish after dish until the circular table is groaning with steamed fish, lemon chicken, and barbecued Peking duck. The transition from indifference to excess is complete and Diana rolls her eyes at the feast facing them. She has a healthy appetite but approaches her food like a model, or a ballet

'Numerous men have mistaken the flattery of her attention for flirtation.'

dancer, knowing that her figure is an essential part of her public persona. At formal functions she eats little, pushing a piece of chicken about on her plate. This has lead to numerous myths about her health, rumours fuelled by her sister Sarah's problems with anorexia nervosa and her own drastic weight loss following the birth of Prince William. As Vivienne Parry of Birthright points out, 'She has a good appetite and normally eats in an anteroom before an official lunchtime reception. For obvious reasons it's difficult to meet and eat at the same time.'

At Mr Wings Diana and her friends try to do justice to the banquet. After two hours the Princess makes her reluctant departure, bowed out by the smiling *maître d'* and his staff.

Today she is celebrated around the globe, everything from the state of her marriage to the shape of her nose is the subject of endless fascination. However, her friends still see the same considerate girl with a finely tuned sense of humour they knew from those carefree days in well-heeled obscurity. She is a loyal friend first, a member of the royal family second.

Since entering the world of royalty, Diana has learned to value her friendships. The pressures of Court life and the presence of photographers can soon untie the bond of companionship. So when she is photographed off-duty she feels more concerned about the impact on her friends than

Above: At official banquets she has the reputation of pushing food around her plate which has given rise to concern about her health.

Below: Even when she goes for a drive on a day off, the Princess is never alone. She is always accompanied by her armed Scotland Yard bodyguard.

herself. She has grown used to the daily deluge. For example, she recently visited the apartment of Old Etonian James Gilbey, the third son of the famous gin distilling family. She stayed until the early hours chatting to her chum. A photographer was waiting outside, the story made front-page news and once again the royal marriage came under the spotlight while Gilbey was besieged at the Saab car showroom where he works.

The reality was rather different. Diana, who has known Gilbey for years, was serving up a little homespun advice to the dark-haired bachelor who had got himself into something of an emotional mess. 'It was more a case of him crying on her shoulder than the other way round,' observes a mutual pal. Diana was aware of the risks involved and was prepared to accept the outcome because of her allegiance to a friend.

The Princess puts a high premium on loyalty and repays that with her friendship and trust. Traditionally the royal family have looked to the aristocracy to form a tight circle around them. The Princess has inevitably followed that pattern so that the social mix of her Court has changed little since that of the 1890s when the then Prince and Princess of Wales dominated smart Society from their grand establishment at Marlborough House.

She plays tennis at the Vanderbilt Club in west London with Julia Dodd Noble (known as Crown Jewels because of her friendship with Diana and Fergie) and Antonia, Marchioness of Douro, who hosted a weekend for the Prince and Princess at the Wellington estate in Spain. Vivacious Kate Menzies, the daughter of a millionaire publishing wholesaler, organizes discreet bridge supper parties where Diana chats to friends like property developer Ben Holland Martin, Major David Waterhouse, the Duke of Marlborough's nephew, and Mervyn Chaplin, who works for Gerard Holdings in the City.

'The Princess puts a high premium on loyalty and repays that with her friendship and trust.'

Naturally Diana's Court features her former flatmates Carolyn Bartholomew and Virginia Pitman while other lunchtime companions include Milly Soames, the daughter of the Lord Lieutenant of Herefordshire, Catherine Soames, the estranged wife of the Conservative MP and a member of the Churchill clan, and Lady Romsey, who lives at the late Lord Mountbatten's stately home of Broadlands in Hampshire.

These days she sees the Duchess of York less frequently. They are no longer the great companions of old as the Duchess, who is busy building her own Household, house, family and royal career, has little time to pay court to the Princess. While they once described their relationship as wonderful, the Princess no longer speaks of her friend with as much warmth. Despite this Diana tried to cheer up her friend during the Duchess's difficult second pregnancy, when Andrew was away at sea and Hector Barrantes, the stepfather she adores, discovered he had cancer. They had a running bet about the sex of the Duchess's second child. Diana wagered it would be a boy called Elvis. Fergie

The Princess is loyal to her circle of friends. She helped the Duchess of York through a tricky second pregnancy and enjoyed a running joke with her sister-in-law about the baby's sex.

knew in her heart she would have a girl. The mother's instinct proved correct.

While many of Diana's circle come from the aristocracy or monied set, Diana is unusual in that her friendships transcend traditional class barriers. When her chef Mervyn Wycherley – known as Seth by Diana – invited her to a lunch at his apartment she was delighted to accept. She was joined by a number of junior officers from the Royal Protection Group who savoured the delights of the royal chef's cordon bleu cookery and admired his elegant drawing room. It is hard to imagine any other member of the royal family agreeing to be entertained by a relatively lowly member of staff. The Queen only sees her chef, Peter Page, once a year when he carves the turkey at lunch on Christmas Day. Such is Diana's interest in the well-being of her staff that when the marriage of her former

number two chef, Graham Newbold, was in trouble, the Princess paid for a holiday so that the couple could try to reconcile their problems. Unfortunately her gesture failed and Graham not only left his wife but also Diana and now works in a premier Scottish hotel.

Mervyn Wycherley's colleague, butler Harold Brown, from Perth, Western Australia, is another of Diana's staff who enjoys more than a purely professional relationship. He joined the royal couple when his predecessor, Alan Fisher, who was more used to the excitements of life with Bing Crosby, left amid a flurry of complaints that the Wales 'were boring'. However, Harold, an active member of the Plymouth Brethren religious sect who takes his Bible everywhere, adores his life in royal service and has a special affection for the Princess. Diana is happy to drop in to his grace-and-favour flat in Kensington Palace and take tea with him as she admires his large collection of Victorian postcards.

He occupies a unique place in her life. Usually, he is the first man she will see in the morning when he gently knocks on the door of her second-floor bedroom with her tea tray. The Princess, already wearing her black and yellow track suit, has a quick drink before driving to Buckingham Palace for her morning swim. For her thirty lengths of breast stroke are a vital relaxation, a time to summon her reserves for the day ahead.

Forty minutes later Diana, her hair only towel dry, returns to 'K.P.' as it is universally known. The Palace, built by Sir Christopher Wren and birthplace to Queen Victoria and Queen Mary, is a unique royal condominium. It is the home for four royal Households – the Prince and Princess of Wales who live at apartments 8 and 9, Prince and Princess Michael of Kent, their neighbours at number 10, Princess Margaret who lives across the courtyard at number 1A and her neighbours, the Duke and Duchess of Gloucester.

With its gas lamps, quiet courtyards and mellow red brick, Kensington Palace has the feel of an elegant English village. However the royal villagers, surrounded by security cameras and patrolling policemen, are not the friendliest of neighbours. The royals are not a 'dropping in'

Kensington Palace is the London home of four royal families. It still retains an air of a pictureque English village in spite of the ever-present police and security cameras.

family and rarely socialize with each other, preferring to communicate through their various private secretaries.

Apartments 8 and 9, initially built for the Duchess of Kendal, mistress to George I, were bomb damaged during World War II and renovation only started in 1975 after the Queen saw at first hand how this Grade One listed building had fallen on hard times. When the Wales moved in it was planned to make their apartment both a home and an office. Their large and growing Household has meant that they have offices two miles away at St James's Palace but inevitably Kensington Palace has also become very much a working home. An endless stream of visitors arrive at their black-painted front door. Charity officials, Palace staff and friends all make their way past the security post to the northwest wing of the Palace which is the weekday home to the Wales.

A regular early bird is Diana's Scottish hairdresser, Richard Dalton, who is a familiar sight, arriving in a black London taxi at 8.30 a.m. from his nearby mews home. Like her chef and butler, 'Mr Richard' has become not just an employee but a friend. A man of gossipy humour, he is one of the few people who is able to joke her out of one of her moody silences. Although he has a salon at Claridges Hotel and a client list which includes Pakistani Prime Minister

Benazir Bhutto, Estée Lauder and Princess Ira von Furstenberg, his first loyalty is to Diana.

He says, 'Basically I plan my life around the Princess's diary. I could be required to go to the Palace at any time, morning or night, weekends, holidays – you name it, I'll be there.' When she returned from a holiday in Majorca, where she was the guest of the King of Spain, Diana immediately called Dalton and asked him to sort out her hair. Dalton dropped everything, left a notice on the salon door saying, 'Sorry, gone snipping,' and went round to his favourite client.

Diana is happy to pay for the privilege – over the last ten years she has spent around £100,000 ($170,000) on hairdressing at home – and there are times when Dalton is almost a permanent fixture in the Princess's dressing room which adjoins the master bedroom.

It is here that Diana, wearing her pink towelling dressing gown or floral kimono, sits in front of her cream kidney-shaped dressing table with its triple mirrors and ponders over her outfits for forthcoming royal engagements, the breakfast show on Capital Radio accompanying their discussions. Dalton, whose mentor is the master Parisian stylist Alexandre, is a powerful influence. 'I think hair should always be part of a total look,' he says, advising her on make-up and

Below: **The Princess with her trusted hairdresser, Richard Dalton. She respects his keen eye for the latest fashion details.**

Opposite: **Diana's swept-back hairstyle has become as distinctive a trademark as her startling blue eyes. Dalton frequently sees her three times a day and accompanies the Princess on all her overseas visits. He even travels to Balmoral and Sandringham to care for Diana's hair.**

clothes. Just as Alexandre was the creative genius behind Princess Grace of Monaco's chic elegance, so Dalton is the inventive advisor guiding Diana's new international look of casual sophistication.

It is a simple philosophy which starts with the basics. 'It doesn't matter how often you wash your hair – as long as you keep putting back what you've taken out,' says Dalton, who keeps a written record of Diana's daily treatments. As Diana has thick mousy hair and swims every day, he uses plenty of Clairol conditioner but only a thimbleful of vitamin and protein shampoo. Occasionally he uses Shimmer Lights, a special ultra-violet shampoo, which neutralizes any brassy yellow effects from the honey-blonde highlights. Before blow drying he applies Infusium 23, a setting lotion which gives body to Diana's closely cropped hair. He uses two different-sized brushes, a small one to turn the hair under at the nape of the neck and a large one to create a softer effect on top.

As Prince Charles has banned all products containing CFCs – the chemical deemed responsible for the hole in the ozone layer – Dalton applies just a drift of ozone friendly Infusium 23 texturing spray to keep her style in place.

Besides trimming Diana's hair every five or six weeks, Dalton is also called in to cut the thinning locks of the Prince and to give the children a trim. The boys often pop into the bedroom to chat to their mother before leaving for school with their nanny. Sometimes it is the only time she sees them – especially if she has an early morning engagement.

As with most royal children, they have their own self-contained day and night nurseries, complete with kitchen, bathroom and staff bedrooms, where they have meals. The Palace may be a working home but to William and Harry it is a place of adventure.

The boys like to wander round the garages and 'help' hose down the royal limousines or ride up and down the drive on their BMX bikes – just like any ordinary children. However, it is not every boy who can wave his mother off to work by helicopter – William and Harry enjoy seeing the red Wessex take off and land at Perk's Field – or watch his father take the salute during

military parades. Indeed William, who is already showing his inclination towards the armed services, enjoys standing by the front door and saluting his father as he leaves for royal engagements. The young Prince learned about saluting and marching from his uncle, Prince Andrew – much to the amusement of guards on duty at Windsor Castle where the lessons took place.

Before he went to his first school, Wetherby, which Harry now attends, William genuinely had no idea that he was a Prince. Diana had always told him that photographers were only present to take her picture, not his. This innocence did not last long. Within a week of starting school his fellow pupils left him in no doubt as to his position. The effect was immediate. There were several instances where he stood in a doorway at Kensington Palace and told visitors, 'You can't go past, I'm Prince William.' Staff soon worked out suitable rejoinders. 'Ah, I'm the Queen of the May' or 'I'm the King of Siam', they retorted. The Prince, after consultations with his nanny, would then reluctantly allow them to carry on.

At Kensington Palace Prince William loves racing around the courtyards on his BMX bike.

Prince William's fellow pupils soon made him aware of his future station in life which, for a time, caused some problems.

Prince William's grandfather, Earl Spencer, observes, 'I think there is a lot of me in him. He's very high spirited, tremendously energetic and always getting into trouble. But you cannot get annoyed with him, however naughty he's been, because he's got such charm. And he's so entertaining with the things he says.'

Now that William is a weekly boarder at Ludgrove School, the royal apartments are quieter. Although the boys are sometimes a noisy presence, they do not trespass too much on the routine of their parents. Charity executive Roger Singleton noted this attitude when he arrived for lunch with the Princess. Although he was greeted at the front door by the Princes he says, 'The children happened to be playing there. They went upstairs with us and then they were off. There was a normality about it. In an ordinary household children don't intrude when

their parents have visitors. You know they are around but they are playing elsewhere.'

While hairdresser Richard Dalton dotes on the two boys, they are not allowed too frequently to attend the main business in hand, Diana's coiffure. When he has packed his brushes away, the Princess goes downstairs for her breakfast in the dining room. Just as Dalton keeps a diary about Diana's hair, so too chef Mervyn Wycherley notes down her choices for the week's meals in a leather-bound menu book. (At Buckingham Palace this procedure is now high tech – the Queen makes her choice from a display on her office computer.)

As with other royal Households, the Prince and Princess breakfast separately, opening their private mail – distinguished from other letters by a secret code at the bottom left-hand corner of the envelope – in between reviewing their typed diaries for the day and glancing at *The Times* newspaper. Such are the demands of their schedules that even if both the Prince and Princess are at home during the day they will only

see each other briefly and the Prince's visitors often have the impression that Diana is not in.

The diary rules every corner of Diana's life. Detailed records about the Princess are kept not only by her chef and hairdresser but also by her dressers, Fay Appleby and Evelyn Dagley. They have several leather volumes to record the date, place and occasion for every dress in the royal wardrobe. It is a necessary function. The Princess now has more than 750 outfits worth over £1.1 million ($1.9 million), among them nearly one hundred evening gowns. Indeed, if her wardrobe were laid end to end it would easily stretch all the way round Kensington Palace.

Diana's clothes are hung on padded hangers in cream cotton bags embossed with her personal cypher and stored in two huge walk-in wardrobes.

Diana gives her cast-offs to her sisters, Sarah Fellowes and Jane McCorquodale. When Diana and her sisters returned to their old school, West Heath *(below)*, Jane made good use of a dress first worn by Diana in Australia *(opposite)*.

Each outfit is carefully tagged with a label detailing when and where it was last worn. Occasionally this meticulous system breaks down. From time to time both her sisters pick out several of Diana's old dresses and wear them frequently in public. Diana says ruefully, 'Sometimes I simply can't find a dress because my sister has borrowed it.'

'A royal dresser is a female Jeeves, interpreting her principal's moods, second-guessing her desires and acting as a diplomatic go-between.'

The dresser's job is far more than monitoring the royal wardrobe, washing the royal underwear and carrying out repairs on her clothes. As the Queen's legendary dresser Bobo MacDonald has proved, they can be the power behind the throne. A dresser is a female Jeeves, interpreting her principal's moods, guessing her wishes and acting as a diplomatic go-between. Like Charles's valets, Diana's dressers see the worst and best of her. They have learned to shrug off her moods, smoothing the feathers of ruffled staff. 'It's not you she is getting at,' Evelyn will soothe when Diana has stalked silently along a Palace corridor, ignoring all and sundry. While Diana can be a temperamental boss, it is noticeable that both women have been with the Princess since the day she started her royal career. 'They adore her,' said one colleague and Diana has repaid that trust.

While the royals and their staff do not normally meet socially, the Princess as we have seen has been the exception to this tradition. In 1987 she attended Fay's wedding to an RAF orderly and was the first to learn that she had cancer and might die. When Fay became too weak to work, Diana insisted that she stay on in her Kensington Palace flat – rather than travel from RAF Benson in Oxfordshire where her husband was based – as it was convenient for her treatment at St Bartholomew's Hospital. On one occasion Diana accompanied her. Fay, now out of danger, has nothing but praise for the support of her employer. 'She gave me encouragement to carry

on,' says Fay. 'She is a lovely person to work for and very special to me.'

Such a close, almost intuitive working relationship enables Diana's dressers to correctly interpret the outfit she will wear – even when the block capitals PRIVATE appear on her daily diary. They will know if she is playing tennis, having lunch or going shopping and pick out an appropriate outfit.

If Diana has a day free from official engagements she will take Prince Harry to school or drive the 800 yards to the English National Ballet rehearsal rooms just behind the Royal Albert Hall. Last year Princess Margaret handed over the patron's baton and since then Diana has followed the company's chequered history – their dance director Peter Schaufuss left abruptly – with considerable interest. The Princess, her detective by her side, will spend an hour watching the dancers as they go through a rehearsal and then join them for coffee afterwards. Quite frequently she takes part herself, changing into a pink leotard and woollen leggings before working out at the bar.

Her teenage ambition to be a ballerina is well known – she grew too tall to qualify – and she still enjoys keeping abreast of the gossip from the ballet world. 'She loves the art form and it gives the dancers a real boost to know that the Princess is so interested,' says one ENB official. Indeed, she has spoken of her wish to write and choreograph her own ballet. Her enjoyment of dance developed during her schooldays as did her enthusiasm for tennis. She played on the courts at Althorp, her Northamptonshire home, although her partners recall that she was not particularly competitive. 'As I grew older I realized I would never be good enough but I still love the game,' she says.

The Princess is a social player. Her personal coach is owner of the Vanderbilt Club, Old Etonian Charles Swallow, who has improved her game out of all recognition. Once she suffered

Opposite: **The Princess has accumulated a wardrobe worth over £1.1 million ($1.9 million). She has more than 90 evening gowns worth nearly £200,000 ($340,000) which are kept in huge wardrobes at Kensington Palace and cared for by two full-time dressers.**

from a weak backhand and a patball serve but now she often deceives her opponents by retrieving balls which they assumed were winners. Even Steffi Graf, who partnered her during a charity match, was impressed. 'She has a good serve and forehand but her backhand needs a little work.'

The Princess is officially involved with two ballet companies and enjoys attending gala evenings. She once had dreams of becoming a dancer but now contents herself with privately taking part in ballet rehearsals.

Diana emerges from the exclusive Vanderbilt tennis club after losing in the second round of the Cartier ladies' doubles charity tournament. Along with swimming, tennis is a favourite sport.

Club members, who include Adam Faith, John McEnroe and Dustin Hoffman, hardly raise an eyebrow when the Princess arrives to play on one of the eight enclosed indoor courts. It was the club's discretion which decided Diana to enrol Prince William, who is 'mad keen', for weekly lessons with their coach, Mandy Sargent.

From time to time the Princess will invite her partner for lunch in the club's dining room. However, her favoured watering holes are nearer home. Beauchamp Place – part of the so-called 'tiara triangle' bounded by Harrods and Harvey Nichols in Knightsbridge – is home to two of her regular restaurants, San Lorenzo and Ménage à Trois. These eateries are chic but anonymous and many tourists have walked by the narrow entrance of San Lorenzo never realizing that Diana was enjoying a chef's salad in the basement below.

It is a place of personalities where Hollywood stars like Sylvester Stallone, Jane Fonda and Goldie Hawn rub shoulders with the likes of Mick Jagger and Rod Stewart when they are in town. On one occasion the Princess was seated at a table with her back to Joan Collins. Neither

The discreet Ménage à Trois restaurant in Knightsbridge is one of Diana's favoured lunchtime haunts.

saw the other but as the lunch progressed they recognized their different voices at the same time. Almost in unison they both turned round, smiled, nodded and carried on their respective conversations. 'It was an interesting piece of social theatre,' recalls one waiter. 'The Queen of Hollywood meets the future Queen of England.'

In the school holidays the Princess likes to treat her children to lunch. As a Christmas treat she took them to the appropriately named Diana's Café where the boys donned paper party hats as they tucked into a plate of buns and cakes, washed down with orange juice. On another occasion she stood in line with other mothers when they visited the Chicago Rib Shack restaurant near Harrods for hamburger and pizza.

Occasionally she will break out of the 'tiara triangle' and head east to fashionable Covent Garden and Soho, once London's infamous red light district. This is the stomping ground of the theatre crowd and her forays to Italian restaurants like Luigi's near the Opera House, or to the trendy Groucho Club, tend to make her detectives edgy. It is something of a security headache with slow-moving traffic and curious tourists milling around.

While the Princess enjoys lunches outside the confines of Kensington Palace, it is often easier all round if she entertains at home. These days she frequently hosts private working lunches for charity officials, digesting the nuances of new policy as she nibbles her quails' eggs and caviar or medaillons of monkfish.

Visitors are greeted at the front door by butler Harold Brown, standing on an expanse of green and grey carpet patterned with the Prince of Wales feathers. On the left is a visitors' book on a Regency mahogany table. The first signature, dated 20 May 1982, is signed 'Spencer (Daddy)' and he is a frequent visitor, as is Diana's sister Jane, who is married to the Queen's deputy private secretary Robert Fellowes – they have a grace-and-favour apartment nearby.

As Diana's luncheon guests follow Harold Brown up the broad staircase, they will notice the eighteenth-century masterpieces – on loan from the Queen's Collection – and John Ward's delightful study of the Princess in her wedding gown. They enter the drawing room, where the

A working lunch at Kensington Palace was the inspiration behind Diana's first major speech which she made on behalf of Barnardo's.

royal couple formally entertain guests who can range from Prime Minister Margaret Thatcher to Space Shuttle astronauts. A £7,000 ($11,900) Broadwood piano, a wedding gift, and a Flemish tapestry depicting a harvest scene dominate the room.

Normally guests chat over a drink for about ten minutes before going into lunch in the dining room next door. It was during such a lunch that the Princess suggested that she make the first major speech of her life. She put forward the idea when she met Tessa Baring, of the illustrious banking family, and Roger Singleton of Barnardo's to discuss their policy for the coming year. As Roger Singleton outlined their plans, Diana asked how she could participate. 'In what sort of way – like making a speech?' asked the Princess in what seemed to be a spontaneous gesture. Her offer was accepted with alacrity and the result was an eloquent and heartfelt appeal for the values of family life which made front-page news and helped establish the charity's new image.

While these exciting plans were discussed Harold Brown and a footman organized the three-course meal unobtrusively. Roger Singleton recalls, 'There was nothing elaborate about

Right: The Princess so
admired designer David
Sassoon's sketch that she
wore his tailored two-piece
suit for the traditional church
service at Sandringham. 'She
has an instantly recognisable
style,' he says. 'It is more
minimal and polished than in
the early days.'

Below: Designer Gina
Fratini's gowns captured the
fairy-tale quality of Diana at
the beginning of her royal
career. Gina, who has
remained in royal favour,
made this evening dress for a
banquet in Auckland, New
Zealand.

the lunch. There was no question of worrying about which knife and fork to use or what glass to drink from. It was not over the top but well done. Obviously it is an enormously exciting occasion and you are not quite sure what is going to happen next. But the equerry and lady-in-waiting are there to help the conversation along and make sure that people relax.'

'The wheels of Diana's life are not always smoothly oiled and there are last-minute panics.'

Indeed the ability to put visitors at ease while keeping to a tight timetable is one of the finer arts of the royal family and its courtier class. So while Diana seems to have all the time in the world as she shows her guests to the front door she knows instinctively that five minutes after the lunch has ended she may have a 2.20 p.m. appointment with her dress designer or her private secretary.

The wheels of the Princess's life are not always so smoothly oiled and there are last-minute panics such as when hatmaker Graham Smith dropped everything to make a cossack hat for the Princess just a couple of days before a State visit. Clothes are important to the Princess and the way she wears them speaks volumes about her character. She spends much time in fittings, choosing fabrics and contemplating designs.

Often two of the men in her life, William and Harry, have the final say. 'That looks nice, Mummy' or 'That looks lovely,' they will comment when she takes them to see her urbane hatmaker Philip Somerville at his Mayfair salon. 'They are extremely well-behaved children,' comments Somerville. 'How many children would sit quietly on a chair watching mum try on lots of hats?' He was delighted when Harry gave him a handwritten note from his mother thanking him for his efforts during Ascot week. Diana likes her designers to be witty and entertaining and Somerville certainly lives up to the billing.

It is a far cry from the fussing and fretting at Buckingham Palace when a vendeuse makes the regular Tuesday call on the Queen. When a designer visits Diana at Kensington Palace he will be more concerned about tripping over a young Prince hiding behind the door than falling down on his Court etiquette. In the past Diana enjoyed visiting her numerous designers in their salons. She telephoned herself, made an appointment and was on her way. The dead hand of security has altered that, especially after several instances when the curious stood with their noses pressed to the shop window watching the Princess.

Normally Diana allocates twenty minutes for a designer like Bruce Oldfield and his assistant. Sketches are spread out on the floor of her study, a cosy north-facing room filled with family photographs and mementoes from her schooldays, while Diana makes her choice. Her dressers take notes and make suggestions, telling the designer when the garment will be worn.

The English designer David Sassoon, who made her outfit for her visit to Sandringham parish church on Christmas Day 1988, explained the procedure. 'If the Princess wants a totally new design we start with a sketch and fabric samples. The rules are simple – no constricting or difficult clothes. When we have agreed on the sketch and fabric, a *toile* is created. This is a practice version made from muslin or calico. You make all your mistakes on a *toile* so that the actual garment looks fresh and clean. The fabric hasn't been tired by too much handling and pinning. Then the corrected *toile* with its markings and tacks makes a master pattern for the outfit. That way we keep fittings to a minimum.'

Although the mechanics of dressing Diana have become more streamlined and professional, she has not lost the human touch. Her small coterie of designers – Catherine Walker and Victor Edelstein the mainstays – have become friends. Dark-haired Catherine, a French-born philosophy student who took up dressmaking as therapy when her English husband was tragically killed, is the creative mind behind many of the Princess's most memorable outfits, notably the ice-blue Hollywood-style gown she wore for the Cannes Film Festival in 1987 and the Mary Queen of Scots evening dress she wore to the Garrard's charity evening in 1987.

Catherine Walker first came to prominence when she designed Diana's black-veiled dress for her meeting with the Pope ('the only time when the Prince and Princess have been really fazed,' recalls an aide). Since then she has forged a close bond with her royal mentor. 'The Princess of Wales has such elegance, grace and *joie de vivre*,' Walker says. 'She does not want to be dressed to look English or French, but to be suitable for her own life.'

However, Diana's groomed but gently witty tailoring owes more to Princess Grace and Hollywood than royal tradition. As David Sassoon observes, 'The Princess has pared down her look. It is more minimal and polished than in the early days. She has discovered that less means more. She now has an instantly recognizable style.' It is a style she has worked for. While the Queen and the Princess Royal rarely set foot inside a Knightsbridge store, the Princess finds shopping a relaxation and an escape. However, her frequent shopping trips are not simply a personal pleasure but a necessary duty. With ten godchildren, numerous weddings and other family occasions to remember, servicing the Court of the Princess of Wales demands time, thought and energy.

'Is it too tight?' she will ask her detective when she appears from a changing room in one of London's trendier boutiques. He nods. 'Good, then I'll buy it,' she says firmly; Chief Inspector Graham Smith then fishes out the Duchy of

Diana with Chief Inspector Graham Smith.

Cornwall American Express credit card from his wallet to pay for the leopard-print dress by outrageous designer Patrick Kelly.

A fashion advisor is just one of the functions of her Scotland Yard 'minders'. As a breed they are straight, stolid and to the point, a sardonic antidote to the obsequious sycophants who swarm round the royal family. They are the only men who are allowed to order her around and often the only ones with the nerve to tell her the off-colour jokes she so enjoys.

She remembers their birthdays, at the end of royal tours sends notes to their wives saying, 'I'm sorry I had to borrow your husband for so long,' and even visits their homes. Her happy knack of befriending staff is in sharp contrast to Charles, who calls his bodyguards by their numbers in times of trouble. 'Where's number one? Where's number one?' he shouted during a skiing trip when he was confronted by paparazzi photographers in an Austrian village, his minder nowhere to be seen.

Although Diana cherishes her time without her shadows, they do have their uses. Charles once ticked her off for continually parking her car on double yellow lines in Knightsbridge when she went shopping. Now her detective deals with over-zealous parking wardens and often has the final say about the socks and shirts she buys for her husband. There are limits, however, as one bodyguard discovered when the Princess bought two designer outfits from Joseph, a store where the staff are better dressed than the customers. The screening computer refused his American Express card so the shop had to send the bill on to Kensington Palace.

There is no fuss or formality when Diana hits the streets, unlike several pop superstars. As the manager of one Kensington store observes, 'She just walks in. We are not pre-warned and she never insists on any special treatment. She has lovely manners, not like some of the big stars. The Princess never asks for the doors to be locked, she just gets on with it. When Madonna came in here she insisted that the doors were closed. Of course, that drew a crowd and stopped the traffic.'

Even if she behaved like a royal prima donna it is debatable whether she would prick characteristic British reserve. When she popped in to the

'Is it too tight?' Diana asked her bodyguard when she emerged from a fitting-room in one outfit. She always takes her minders on shopping expeditions.

W.H. Smith bookstore in Kensington to buy Judith Krantz's blockbuster, *Scruples*, she gaily asked the assistant if he had seen her on the television the previous evening. 'No,' he replied, 'there was something better on the other side.'

His nonchalance was understandable. Diana's former nanny Ruth Wallace often took her royal charges on shopping excursions near to the Palace while the Princess is seen so frequently in Kensington that the main shopping thorough-fare has been nicknamed 'Kensington Di Street'. On Friday afternoon the Princess, casually dressed in jeans and headscarf, regularly drops into Safeway supermarket and stocks up on

When she goes shopping for her boys she regularly buys two of everything in case they squabble.

last-minute purchases before heading down the M4 motorway to Highgrove. 'I wheel my trolley along and no one takes any notice of me,' she says. 'I like to choose health food for the boys' tea but they prefer things that are bad for them, I'm afraid.'

During the week the local Marks and Spencer store is favoured. She buys white bread and muffins to make the bacon sandwiches she so enjoys. Peach bubble bath and bras have also been on her shopping list. One eagle-eyed assistant noted, 'The last time she came was with two detectives. She must have been hungry because she walked upstairs eating a packet of spring onion crisps which she had bought in the food hall.'

The street is also convenient for children's clothes and toys. She is a valued customer at the junior Benetton store where at the start of the season she stocks up on cardigans, sweatshirts and cord trousers. 'I always have to buy two of everything otherwise they squabble,' she says. Occasionally she calls in at the Children's Book Centre to add to the boys' bookshelves. The adventures of Babar the elephant, Diana's own childhood favourite, and Winnie the Pooh, as well as Enid Blyton, can be seen in their nursery. She says, 'I have to be careful I don't give them scary books for bedtime reading.' However she couldn't resist Alan Baker's book, *One Naughty Boy*, about a mischievous youngster with an uncanny resemblance to Prince William who creates mayhem in a wildflower garden remarkably similar to the one at Highgrove.

After the Book Centre she pops along to a branch of the Body Shop to replenish her supplies of peppermint foot lotion – so soothing after a long day – as well as their raspberry bath salts, eyelash combs and concealer sticks. Then she heads to Kensington Church Street to Crabtree and Evelyn for the store's own brand of honey or small Christmas gifts like the corgi-shaped soaps which she bought for the Queen. Their range of Tom Kitten toiletries goes down well with her nephews and nieces.

While she does have favourite stores – Harvey Nichols, Harrods and the General Trading Company – she is quite happy dropping into shops such as the Kensington High Street branch of Ravel, a middle-market shoe chain, to buy a pair of £40 ($68) flat shoes before flying up to Balmoral, and then paying £85 ($145) for a red and white baseball jacket from Slick Willy's, which stocks trendy Americana.

Her private purchases reveal the Princess's hidden personality. Many of the clothes she buys never see the light of day in public and would create a sensation if she ever wore them to a royal function. She certainly raised the eyebrows of several stallholders when she wandered into Kensington Market and bought a red PVC skirt and she regularly browses through the racks at Hyper Hyper, couturiers to outrageous café society.

Her off-duty style could be characterized as sensual masculinity: velvet trousers teamed with

'Her off-duty style could be characterized as sensual masculinity.'

a satin bow-tie and evening jacket, red leather trousers or a black leather skirt and a satin bomber jacket. 'I do like men in uniform,' she says, incorporating her preferences into her private wardrobe. A cricket sweater by the American designer Ralph Lauren and a man's hacking jacket were summer favourites.

When she is on parade Diana wears British labels, privately she prefers slinky silks by the Italian Valentino, outfits from Kenzo of Paris and dresses by Gianni Versace, whom she met after an evening at La Scala opera house in Milan. Occasionally, she slips into Valentino's Bond Street store and heads downstairs to the evening-wear department. She has several Valentino party outfits which she wears for lunches and dinners at weekend house parties. Prince Charles's particular favourite is a white silk blouse with organza collar which she wears with a grey satin beaded skirt.

Nevertheless she is not entirely unpatriotic in private. She rifles through the clothes racks at Simpson's of Piccadilly looking at the latest offerings by Paul Costelloe and Caroline Charles. Costelloe, a personable Irishman with five young children, is another of the designers accepted at Diana's Court. He says, 'My clothes must be the least expensive of her purchases but she never asks the price. I meet the Princess privately and hold her in great esteem, far more than some of the other royals I have met.'

She spends around £2,000 ($3,400) a week on clothes for herself and another £600 ($1,020) on accessories like belts, handbags, and shoes. Most of her off-duty footwear comes from Pied à Terre, a smart store specializing in handmade Italian footwear on Sloane Street near the General Trading Company – the shopping mecca for the town and country set.

Sensual masculinity characterizes Diana's private wardrobe. She likes jeans or trousers and has been known to borrow her husband's jackets.

51

'She wants to be treated like anyone else,' say staff, who know that she always requests 'comfortable' casuals, costing £120 ($204), by Pancaldi for her size 6½ feet. For her on-duty shoes she visits Charles Jourdan, who give her their preferential executive service which is reserved for their most exclusive clientele. She visits twice a year to view the latest collections, slipping upstairs to the wholesale floor. While she spends around £100 ($170) a pair – and in the last decade she has bought around 350 pairs of shoes – the Princess likes them to last. When Prince Charles's dog Tigger chewed one pair they were promptly dispatched for repair to Rayne's, the official Court cobblers.

Time and security considerations mean that she rarely has a chance to browse. Instead she uses her ladies-in-waiting as 'scouts' to hunt out thoughtful gifts for her friends and family. Diana's diary is filled with birthdays as well as wedding invitations and anniversaries. Each Christmas she has to dream up presents for at least fifty relatives – and that's before she starts thinking about her friends. Little wonder then that Christmas starts early for the Princess – she boasts that she has finished her shopping by October.

She finds gifts for christenings, her godchildren and nieces from the fashionable Anthea More Ede in Launceston Place, or the White House in Bond Street, probably the most expensive children's store in Britain.

With velvet-collared coats at £425 ($723) and the handsmocked dresses costing £250 ($425), it is as well that Diana is as generous as she is considerate. Gifts for wedding presents are usually purchased from the General Trading Company although Diana occasionally visits Tiffany in Old Bond Street to choose from their selection of modern gold jewellery, silverware and photograph frames.

Birthdays are trickier. Enamel boxes from Halcyon Days, who also make her official gifts for foreign tours, are a favoured standby as is fun jewellery from Butler and Wilson. A couple of days after buying a glass spider brooch and matching earrings for herself she returned to buy two further sets for her friends. 'They will think they are a great joke,' she told staff. She likes presents to be apposite and where possible amus-

Presents loom large in Diana's life. Unlike other members of the royal family, she likes to buy gifts for her friends and family herself.

ing, favouring stores like Present Affairs and Frog Hollow (where she adds to her collection of reptiles) for gift ideas. Even when a present is simply a box of chocolates, she invests it with some style. Last Christmas she ordered a £55 ($94) box of Charbonnel et Walker selection for her mother.

While the royal family is notoriously prudent when buying presents – Charles once told Diana off for buying him an expensive dinner jacket for Christmas – her circle of friends repays her generosity with interest. They buy her tasteful Russian trinkets, jewellery and antique boxes from discreet, high-class and well-established merchants. The offerings truly befit the style of a future queen. For example at Hancocks in Burlington Gardens, who hold the royal warrant for the Queen Mother, friends have bought her antique silverware while others favour Ermitage, which specializes in Fabergé and other Russian *objets d'art*. Prices start from £1,500 ($2,550) for a silver-topped glass flacon although a Fabergé leaves little change out of £5,000 ($8,500) for the smallest carving.

'There are chivalrous gallants who spend thousands on jewellery and antiques for the Princess.'

Then there are the chivalrous gallants who regularly spend thousands of pounds on jewellery and antiques for the Princess. A charming, discreet bachelor often visits Mr Hill, the manager of Eckstein, a tasteful antique shop once frequented by Queen Mary. On his visits to the Jermyn Street shop he buys Diana eighteenth-century antiques including enamelled boxes. Just before Christmas, Diana's mysterious benefactor paid £2,500 ($4,250) for a charming antique *bonbonnière* or sweet dish. The unusual piece had a King Charles spaniel resting on a cushion for a lid.

Diana's friends buy her expensive presents which reflect her status. She wore this £2,200 ($3,740) pearl and diamond bracelet – a gift from a friend – during her visit to Hong Kong.

While many of her presents from her 'courtiers' remain within the privacy of Kensington Palace and Highgrove, the Princess shows no such diffidence with the jewellery bought by friends. She prizes a three-row pearl and diamond bracelet so much that she wore it for the first night of the musical *Miss Saigon* and a banquet in Hong Kong. Jeweller Nigel Milne, who made the £2,200 ($3,740) bracelet, is naturally flattered by Diana's enjoyment of his designs, some of which were made specifically to raise money for the Birthright charity.

Certainly Prince Charles would think twice about spending so lavishly on jewellery for the Princess. Recently he accepted a necklace from students at the Royal College of Art and then asked jeweller Clarissa Mitchell to show him her other work so that he could choose a piece for his wife. He loved a modern bracelet but blanched when she told him it was £9,000 ($15,300). 'Too expensive,' he said.

This then is the Court of the Princess of Wales. In the last few years she has created a lifestyle which reflects her interests in the arts and sport without compromising the demands of her family and her exalted position. Yet her status has not turned her head. 'What we like most about her is that she has no side,' say numerous friends.

Hers is an urban Court which harks back to Regency times when the pursuits of hunting, shooting and fishing were not the abiding preoccupations of the aristocracy. She values gallantry, charm and repartee more than the ability to jump a five-bar gate at full gallop and she treasures loyalty and openness above place and position. The iconography of her fashion articulates the values of her Court. An awareness of fashion and hence the outside world together with a gentle mockery of the *status quo* reflect the Princess's nature.

She has succeeded in making a stylish personal statement within the highly constricted and conservative royal world. The essential difference is that while the Queen and the Prince of Wales preside over a country Court, the Princess is developing her own metropolitan Court.

If the enjoyment of urban pleasures casts her in the role of a royal rebel, then it is a part that she has the strength and conviction to carry off.

CHAPTER THREE
A Weekend in the Country

A black cat flying through the door at head height is hardly the conventional greeting associated with an arrival at a royal residence. At Highgrove it is a not infrequent occurrence as Prince Charles, who loathes the animals, has a standing instruction that all cats are thrown out immediately. It can be disconcerting for the unwary visitor. Guests are more likely to be admiring the famous wildflower garden planted by Miriam Rothschild which borders the gravel drive than watching out for low-flying cats. Highgrove, set in 353 acres of fertile Gloucestershire countryside a few miles outside the quaint market town of Tetbury, is a surprising choice for the country home of the Queen's eldest son.

It is a square, unprepossessing mansion with none of the grandeur associated with other country retreats. Several years ago Charles tried to remedy that by adding a row of Palladian columns to the front of the house in an attempt to invest it with greater architectural dignity. His efforts at artificially weathering the columns had his gardeners brewing gallons of tea to stain the stone.

This ploy clearly has not worked for the difference in colour can easily be seen from the main road which runs close to the royal residence. Any number of locals are annoyed by drivers who dawdle along the road, straining their necks for a fleeting glimpse of the 200-year-old house. Indeed villagers were surprised when, in 1980, the Prince paid the late Maurice Macmillan, son of the former Prime Minister, the late Lord Stockton, nearly £800,000 ($1.36

million) for the nine-bedroomed house. When he took possession, the Prince, who regularly invited his polo friends to join him in a supper of fish and chips from the local takeaway, did little in the way of renovation or decoration. He expected that he would be showered with presents when he married – and so it has proved.

There is hardly a piece of furniture, a painting or an ornament in the house which was not given to the royal couple on their wedding day. The rest of the furnishings are made up from antiques stored at Windsor Castle, some dating back to George I. The interior has the air of a well-kept country house hotel where the personality and taste of the owners are kept discreetly in the background. Unlike normal houses, there is no room for untidiness, further emphasizing the feeling of walking around a stately home. In every room the presence of 'panic buttons' – only to be used in an emergency – add to the impression of impersonality. There may be roses around the garden gate but there is a security camera hidden in the foliage and a 'panic button' placed behind the blooms. Yet this is home to the Prince and Princess, a rural retreat where the pressures of royal life subside for a time.

While it may be an oasis of calm in a busy life – bored staff call the Wales' home 'Highgrave' – there are still certain formalities to be observed. After all this is the home of the future

Relaxed and carefree, the Princess enjoys the peace and quiet of a cycle ride along a country lane.

Highgrove is the country seat of the Prince and Princess of Wales. Prince Charles has transformed the gardens and added pillars to give the house a 'classical' look. Although there is an open-air swimming pool for Diana, she has to go to a nearby hotel to play tennis.

king and queen. For example, Charles will not allow workmen to wear shorts – even in the height of summer – lest they offend his wife. He has the reputation of being an exasperating employer, a benevolent perfectionist who ordered a brick wall to be demolished just as it was completed because he felt it was too high and yet bought his loyal general factotum, Paddy Whitelands, a dictaphone to help his work when the old man's memory began to fail him.

This fussy formality generates a certain schoolroom atmosphere – there is much illicit merrymaking when the royal principals are away. On one occasion the Union Jack was taken off the flag pole and a bra put in its place; another time a detective performed a late-night streak along the driveway for a bet. His drunken efforts were recorded on a police video camera for posterity.

However, Highgrove, as befitting a properly run country home, gives no sign to the casual visitor of the occasional merrymaking. The first clue to the ownership of the mansion is given when you walk through the front door into the 40-foot-long entrance hall. Prince of Wales feathers decorate numerous objects from the metal boot-scraper to a pair of Regency mahogany hall chairs. A portrait of the Queen painted by Richard Stone in Silver Jubilee year is a further pointer. Above the marble fireplace is a fine Reynolds oil of a squire with his children which the royal couple once loaned to an exhibition of the 'Best of British' painting held in Washington. A Georgian walnut grandfather clock, a gift from the City of Westminster, and a bronze pair of racehorses galloping neck and neck, a wedding present from the Jockey Club, emphasize the standing of the owner, while the 1982 Jaipur Trophy and a bronze sculpture showing the Prince of Wales on horseback playing polo finally leaves the visitor in no doubt as to the identity of the man of the house.

There are feminine touches but they are deceptive. The elegant Regency piano which stands next to Charles's cello in the corner of the polished wooden floor could be used by the Princess who has inherited the musical ability of her grandmother, Ruth, Lady Fermoy. Sadly this is not so. The beautiful tones of the Clementi piano are only heard when the blind piano tuner comes every six months to service it. However, it was Diana, working in conjunction with Dudley Poplak, the couple's South African-born interior designer, who chose the apricot and gold colour scheme – apricot for the walls, terracotta and gold for the swagged curtains. A lovely flower-patterned Kelim rug and two pairs of Limoges and Canton vases soften the essentially masculine feel of the entrance hall.

But perhaps the most striking feature of the entrance hall is the scent of flowers which is a charming feature throughout the house. Lemon geraniums, lilies and six-foot-high jasmine plants are favourites. The Prince proudly tells guests that they are home grown in his greenhouse.

Leading off the entrance hall is the Princess's sitting room, a light and airy room overlooking the garden, where Diana spends her days writing letters or chatting to friends on the telephone. From her mahogany writing desk, once used by Queen Victoria, she can see the boxed hedging with its intertwined 'C' and 'D' – a romantic decorative feature which is visible when the royal couple arrive at Highgrove by helicopter. It is a room which gives many clues to the personality and interests of the occupant. Family photographs – including a large black-and-white picture of Charles in his bachelor days – and paintings predominate. On her desk, next to the freesias which are replenished daily, are pictures of William and Harry in a folding leather frame. She has endless photographs of her friends and family and, a notoriously neat

person, enjoys nothing more on a wet weekend than rearranging them.

A pencil sketch of her grandfather, the 7th Earl Spencer, by Adrian Beach and a watercolour of Althorp by Margo Harrison remind the visitor that Diana's aristocratic roots go deep. Less immediately revealing is a portrait of the poet Lord Byron alongside a sketch of the 3rd Earl Spencer, known by his contemporaries as 'Honest Jack Althorp'. The mystery is explained by the 3rd Earl's friendship with Byron, forged when they were both pupils at Harrow School. 'Honest Jack' later became a successful Leader of the House of Commons, a Liberal Chancellor of the Exchequer and promoter of the First Reform Bill.

There may be roses round the door leading to Charles's garden but beneath the foliage is a 'panic button' which raises the alarm should an intruder enter the grounds.

'The interior has the air of a well-kept country house hotel.'

Besides her ancestry, her interests are also represented. John Ward's painting of the Royal Opera House, Covent Garden, is evidence of Diana's love of ballet. As a teenager she regularly waited at the stage door collecting autographs of the prima ballerinas. When she sat next to the Russian dancer Mikhail Baryshnikov at a White House banquet she reminded him that his signature was in her book. This passion for the arts is reflected in her collection of tapes and records which is stored on either side of the marble fireplace. Recordings of virtually every ballet including *Swan Lake*, *Giselle*, and *Sleeping Beauty* dominate her collection although there is space for the music of rock groups like Dire Straits, Duran Duran, Phil Collins and Billy Joel. While much has been made of her love of pop, in reality ballet and classical music truly represent her taste, further emphasized by her collection of biographies of great composers such as Mozart, Beethoven and Debussy which adorn the deep white shelving facing the fireplace.

Alongside these books is a collection of glassware, mainly wedding gifts. There is a large rummer or drinking glass engraved with an inscription celebrating George III's Jubilee in 1809, a selection of exquisite glass bowls, one engraved with Highgrove House, another with hunting scenes, as well as Derby and Copenhagen plates and coffee cups. The donors are as varied as building societies, the Drapers' Company, HMS *Rothesay* and the islands of Colonsay and Oronsay in Scotland.

However, the one collection she has built up herself consists of charming enamel boxes, many from Halcyon Days, showing Victorian street scenes and country houses as well as one with the legend 'I love you', a gift from Prince Charles.

The sense of cosiness and tranquility which predominates in Diana's study contrasts vividly with the chaos which greets the visitor when entering Charles's study. It is a tiny room, overlooking the patio he helped design and build, and is smothered in paperwork. Business papers relating to the Duchy of Cornwall estates, forthcoming royal engagements, locked blue boxes containing government papers and briefing documents on his numerous charities cover every inch of his mahogany desk and the floor. Sometimes it is extremely difficult to open the door, such is the disorganization within.

Yet in such a small working space he has managed to add several homely touches. A photograph of 'Uncle Dickie' (Lord Mountbatten) and an oil of his grandfather, George VI, together with a pencil sketch by Sir William Beechey of George III, a much misunderstood monarch, hang on the walls. George III has a special fascination for the Prince. He spent weeks delving into the archives at Windsor Castle in an effort to prove that the eighteenth-century monarch was not mad.

A watercolour of Lochnagar, the looming mountain above Balmoral which was the inspiration for his award-winning children's book, *The Old Man of Lochnagar*, as well as Victorian sketches in sepia of grouse moors and Scottish fishing scenes indicate the Prince's sporting interests. With its quill pens, glass ink stands and shelves crammed with signed copies of books on travel, the Navy and history – including Winston Churchill's *History of the English Speaking Peoples* – it is very much a squire's study, the conventional bolt hole for the English country gentleman.

Traditional is the style of the overall decoration of the house, no more so than in the drawing room which is used for entertaining everyone from the Queen Mother to camera crews. The crew of the BBC television programme 'Tomorrow's World' create havoc each year when they arrive to film an awards ceremony. While it is a house rule that all workmen are accompanied by a member of staff, the BBC technicians are a law unto themselves as they roam round the rooms looking for power points for their cables.

While the BBC can make themselves at home, Prince William and Prince Harry are banned from entering the green-carpeted drawing room. The room is decorated in gold, cream and green and contains comfortable three-seater sofas and a pair of easy chairs. There are a number of valuable antiques and porcelain animals on show.

The wildflower garden dominates the approach to Highgrove. It was planted at the suggestion of naturalist Miriam Rothschild.

On the various Regency and Georgian occasional tables are glass bowls engraved with the Prince and Princess's coats of arms, a Derby two-handled vase commemorating the royal wedding, silver boxes, an antique French clock amusingly mounted with a cockerel, a mantel clock from Tiffany's in New York together with a pottery parrot, Nymphenberg horses and riders, Herend porcelain pheasants and a china bullfrog.

The frog motif runs throughout the house and is very much Diana's inspiration based on the legend of the girl who kissed a frog which turned into a Prince. She even has a silver frog mascot on her Ford Escort which she had resprayed green so that the frog looked as though it was sitting in a lake of water lilies.

In common with the drawing room, the dining room is out of bounds to the boys, except on special occasions when, for example, Diana's sister Sarah or her father, Earl Spencer, visit. Normally the boys eat in the nursery with their nanny for the dining room is used only by adults. It is a simple but impressive room dominated by a 66-inch-wide polished mahogany oval dining table which can seat fourteen comfortably. The pink and cream Louis XV dining chairs, which are emblazoned with the distinctive Prince of Wales feathers, are rarely fully occupied. Occasionally when the Prince hosts a working dinner for groups of advisors from the world of architecture, science and agriculture, the dining room will be alive to the buzz of conversation. Often when the Wales entertain their guests will be another couple; King Constantine and Queen Anne-Marie of Greece are regular visitors as is British Airways chairman Lord King.

Dinner guests who use the downstairs bathroom are amused to find the smallest room in the house decorated with newspaper cartoons

'The Princess is a great "snacker" who cannot resist picking at leftovers in the fridge.'

by Giles, Garland and Tugg which relate to Charles's naval career and the royal wedding. Like the dining room, the bathroom is off a long polished-wood corridor, decorated with pen and ink maps and a portrait of Allibar, the steeple-chaser which tragically died while Charles was riding him. The corridor leads to the kitchen and the staff dining room. The kitchen was provided as a wedding present. Indeed the royal couple were given three light-oak German kitchens by various manufacturers and so were able to distribute them among the various staff cottages on the estate. Diana is a frequent visitor to the white-tiled kitchen, discussing the week-end menu with her chef or the housekeeper. Even though there is a dishwasher, she has been known to put on a pair of pink rubber gloves and help with the washing up at the stainless-steel double sink. More often she is caught by staff

The Princess, who is frequently seen on early morning jogs, shows her paces as she races through the daffodils.

late at night as she burgles the fridge. The Princess, who frequently makes herself a bowl of custard before she goes to bed, is a great 'snacker' who cannot resist picking at leftovers in the fridge.

She does deny herself alcohol and the butler's pantry which leads off the kitchen has none of the perks for staff traditionally associated with this room. A bottle of Famous Grouse whisky, Pimm's No. 1 Cup, gin, martini and cherry brandy are the only spirits in the house while wine, usually white, is bought specially for entertaining.

No visit to Highgrove would be complete without an excursion to the cellars. These cavernous rooms answer that most elusive question – what does Diana do with all the weird and wonderful offerings which are given to her? The answer is simple for they end up buried in the cellar. It is filled with boomerangs that will never come back, enough grass skirts to stage a production of *South Pacific*, carved ivory tusks, Mexican sombreros, Maori head dresses and even a green woollen 'willie warmer' which Prince Charles was once given for Christmas.

Retracing his steps from the cellar, along the ground-floor corridor to the entrance hall, the visitor climbs the broad staircase to the first floor. The staircase is so gloomy that, try as he might, the Prince has not been able to encourage any shade-loving plants to survive and has been forced to decorate the half landing with a dried flower arrangement. As may be expected, the landing which leads to the royal bedrooms is quiet, the hush only broken by the ticking of two grandfather clocks, one a wedding present from the people of Portland in Dorset.

On the landing all the furniture is tastefully Georgian, in keeping with the period of the house. The eighteenth-century travelling com-mode, a present from their friends, the Duke and Duchess of Wellington, perfectly complements a pair of Georgian dining chairs which were given by the people of Bermuda.

Leading off the landing, which surrounds a central stairwell, is the master bedroom. This is dominated by a romantic six-foot-wide Georgian mahogany four poster with a red and green silk canopy and drapes, and a cuddly green frog lying on top of the bedspread. Traditionally the royal

'The master bedroom is dominated by a romantic six-foot-wide Georgian four-poster bed.'

Weekends are a time for the Princess to relax with her children. On this occasion Prince Harry enjoys her attention.

couple have sheets, blankets and a quilted bed-spread rather than a duvet.

If Diana's bed is the stuff of fairy tales then the saga of her mattress parallels the story of the Princess and the pea. Years of picking up small children as well as rigorous ballet exercises have strained her back so that she needs a very firm mattress to sleep on. Shortly after she moved into Highgrove the oversized mattress was returned to the Plymouth factory to be resprung.

On either side of the four poster are mahogany bedside tables with a mahogany and brass 'panic button' on the wall above them. They have been used. On one occasion, when Diana was sleeping alone, she thought she heard an intruder moving about outside her window. She quickly pressed the alarm which alerted the patrolling police and the local police headquarters in Cheltenham. As searchlights lit the grounds,

dozens of police and tracker dogs converged on the estate and mounted a futile search into the early hours for the alleged trespasser.

Normally, little disturbs the tranquility of Diana's bedroom. It is a restful room, decorated with charming watercolours and miniatures by artists such as Sir Hugh Casson, John Piper and Raoul Dufy. An indication of Diana's taste in bedtime reading is displayed on top of the Regency chests at either end of the room. Novels by Evelyn Anthony and romances by Danielle Steele, who always sends Diana signed first editions, as well as more intellectual works such as Lady Elizabeth Longford's biography of Queen Victoria, are her staple diet. Diana's passion for animals is also evident. Besides the toy frog on her bed there are Herend porcelain rabbits, a carved china pig and pottery frogs.

Her *en suite* bathroom is one of the prettiest and simplest rooms in the house. She chose pink wallpaper with a trellis design and a white Armitage bathroom suite with gold-plated bath taps. There is no separate shower and Diana makes do with a shower attachment to her bath.

She puts on her make-up sitting in front of a pink triple-mirrored kidney-shaped dressing table which stands next to a five-drawer

Diana has an extra-hard mattress on her four-poster bed. Years of picking up her children has damaged her back and she needs additional support.

mahogany chest where she keeps her white cotton Marks and Spencer and grey silk La Perla underwear as well as tee-shirts, sweatshirts and her swimwear. In the corner of the bathroom is a small built-in wardrobe with louvred doors where she hangs her jeans, trousers and dresses. It is neither as elaborate or extensive as expected – the overwhelming majority of Diana's clothes are kept at Kensington Palace.

On top of the chest of drawers are dozens of knick-knacks from her youth and childhood. Besides the ubiquitous frogs, there is a Beatrix Potter rabbit, engraved silver boxes and memorabilia, including a diving cup from her days at West Heath School. On the wall a picture from the story of King Babar adds to the decorative mood of reminiscence. A watercolour of Windsor Castle by Rosemarie Mackworth-Young, a pair of bird studies by Marjorie Blamey and a watercolour of the 'Frogs' Fishing Party' by Roger McPhail complete the furnishings.

Next door, in Charles's dressing room which he frequently uses as a bedroom, images of childhood are immediately apparent. Tucked in his seven-foot-long sofa bed is a battered teddy, which accompanies him everywhere. It is so ancient that the Queen Mother has sewn back the velvet feet to restore a little of teddy's dignity. Old teddy has a special place in Charles's heart. The Prince insists that his arms are tucked inside the bed sheets at night so that 'he doesn't get cold'. When the Prince travels abroad his valet places teddy in a plastic shirt bag and takes him with the entourage. The only occasions when teddy is left at home are when Charles visits the regiments where he is colonel in chief. It does not accord with his masculine image. While this concern may be considered eccentric, it is not unusual. Both of his brothers, the Duke of York and Prince Edward, have kept their teddies and lavish as much attention on them as Charles does on his.

A watercolour of the Queen Mother when she was Lady Elizabeth Bowes-Lyon, another profound childhood influence, hangs on the wall together with a chalk study of Diana by Molly Bishop, while a tasteful collection of reclining nudes drawn by Duncan Grant, a leading light in the Bloomsbury group and much admired by Charles's grandmother, adds to the impression

of a bachelor's bedroom. The stern mahogany furniture, which ranges from a Pembroke desk used by King George V to an occasional table from the Governor and people of St Helena in the South Atlantic, with a miniature of George III which is displayed above the fireplace, heighten the masculine atmosphere.

When he first viewed the house, Charles was impressed that many of the original features had been retained, especially in his bathroom. He is interested in Victorian plumbing and has several books on the subject. His bathroom is an antique collector's dream with a wooden and marble Victorian lavatory, a marble sink with brass taps and a bath and shower encased in polished mahogany. A snapshot of his active outdoor life is revealed in drawings and watercolours hanging on the green walls. There is a chalk sketch of his polo exploits, a view of the River Hofsa in Iceland where he fishes in winter, South African desert scenes – he has twice enjoyed trekking breaks in the Kalahari Desert – and watercolours of Trinity College, Cambridge, where he studied archeology and anthropology.

Along the landing are the two guest bedrooms and bathrooms, both boasting four-poster beds,

The Duke of York has known Diana since childhood and used Highgrove as a safe haven during his romance with Sarah Ferguson. Their visits are remembered as noisy occasions.

one a wedding gift from the Canadian government. There are pictures of Windsor and Glamis Castles, sepia prints of Edward VII as a child, various polo paintings as well as armchairs emblazoned with the Spencer and Windsor arms and the Prince of Wales feathers. While one of the guest rooms is called the Queen's Bedroom she has never made an overnight visit. In fact, the only member of the immediate royal family to have stayed is Prince Andrew who spent two weekends there with Sarah Ferguson shortly before their engagement. They used Highgrove as a retreat from the Press interest in their romance. Their noisy, high-spirited behaviour shattered the peace and tranquility normally associated with the Prince and Princess.

Equally shattering was the day Lady King knocked over an expensive Chinese vase as she went to open the window in the guest bedroom. 'I could have thrown myself out,' a crest-fallen Lady King told friends afterwards. Fortunately, the vase was painstakingly rebuilt by the china

On a sunny day Diana loves to curl up with a good book in the secluded gardens.

restorer at the Street Farm workshops on the Highgrove estate.

While inquisitive guests are able to take a quick peek into the royal bedrooms to satisfy their curiosity, there is one room on the landing floor which is always kept locked. This is the 'iron room', a steel shelter designed to safeguard the Prince and his family in case of terrorist or nuclear attack. The mahogany door facing the royal bedroom gives no clue as to its purpose. The door is steel-lined and the room itself, which was formerly a bathroom, is austere. Only a couple of chairs and a wall safe relieve the grey metal interior.

While Highgrove is surrounded by a battery of infra-red beams, spy cameras and floodlights, the only alarms so far have been caused by pranks, cranks and the odd fox which breaks the infra-red circuit and triggers a warning in the police

A weekend in the country is a chance for the Princess to unwind away from the cares of London. There are few visitors to the Wales' country estate and only a handful of Diana's friends have ever enjoyed royal hospitality.

post. On one occasion four local youths climbed over the wall and tried to scrape paint off the front door for a dare, while a well-groomed but unbalanced blonde managed to inveigle her way past police at the gate only to be stopped at the front door when she insisted on seeing Prince Charles and tried to force her way in. Police feared the worst when a red Alfa Sud car smashed into the main gates one summer's afternoon. It was not a precursor to a terrorist attack however. The elderly driver had had a heart attack as he passed the entrance to the royal estate and lost control of his car. One of the first on the scene was Prince Charles who thumped the pensioner's chest to revive his heart and used his handkerchief to stem the flow of blood on his injured arm. He was soon taken to hospital where he subsequently recovered.

Security of a different order is apparent on the nursery floor. The central well means that there is a 30-foot drop to the ground. Sensibly Diana insisted that a wire-mesh covering was installed to prevent her boys from climbing over the banisters and falling. With light streaming in through the attic windows (which are also barred for safety), the constant chatter of chil-

dren's conversation, and furnished with pine rather than mahogany, the nursery floor is perhaps the liveliest and most appealing part of the house. For a while the decoration was too lifelike for Harry's taste. Before William was born, Diana commissioned a mural of fourteen different Disney characters for the day nursery. But artist Simon Barnett's outsize figures of Mickey Mouse, Donald Duck and company gave Diana's second son so many nightmares that the walls were repainted in a more neutral beige.

Other pictures, some painted by family friends, are less frightening. Bird scenes by the naturalist Sir Peter Scott, and views of Cornwall and the Isles of Scilly, where the boys have spent several holidays, by the Crown Equerry Sir John Miller, decorate several rooms on the nursery floor. Laura Faitisne's charming watercolour of Prince William hangs over his bed while a chalk study of Harvey, Charles's ancient Labrador, and a picture by Ludmilla Trapp of their father as a three-year-old take pride of place in the day nursery.

The nursery floor is entirely self-contained with a day and night nursery, a nanny's bedroom and bathroom next door, a laundry room and rooms for a Scotland Yard detective and valet. The police headquarters are the meanest in the house and this is because the local police authority had to pay to decorate these rooms, doing so with minimum expenditure. Ironically the attic above is crammed with the most expensive and sophisticated surveillance equipment money can buy.

However, the royal minder does have the use of the cooking facilities and staff dining room on the nursery floor. While their nanny will occasionally make a snack upstairs, normally the boys have their hot meals prepared in the main kitchen. As may be expected from such abstemious parents, they have a healthy, wholesome diet with at least one hot meal a day. Sweets, fizzy drinks and chocolates are only allowed on special occasions, for example when their chef, Mervyn Wycherley, makes them a decorative chocolate egg at Easter. Diana was horrified when she once discovered William sitting on the floor of the kitchen pantry guzzling a bottle of pop. She looked at the list of additives and promptly banned drinks containing sugar.

The Princes, who eat at the pine table in the nursery, normally have a simple breakfast of Rice Krispies or Weetos with brown toast and milk. Lunch can be shepherd's pie or fish fingers with vegetables from the Highgrove garden and a dessert of fruit, yoghurt or *fromage frais*. In the evening beans on toast, a poached egg – provided by the hens which roam round the grounds – or a piece of fish could be on the menu. 'They have nothing special or elaborate,' says a former member of staff. 'The boys have the same plain, ordinary fare enjoyed by other children.'

However, there is nothing understated about the army of toys which they can marshall. From the moment they were born, William and Harry have wanted for nothing. As babies they were surrounded by cuddly toys, colourful mobiles, and squeaky animals. Now they are growing up, the toys which were put away for them have been taken out of the cupboards. Toy soldiers, model tanks, battery-operated helicopters, racing cars, even foxes dressed in polo gear, are their daily delight. William particularly enjoys racing his scale model cars across the beige carpet. He persuaded his mother to take him to the Motorfair and was not put off driving when he suffered a nasty bump steering his own car in the Highgrove courtyard.

The young Prince's fibre-glass £100,000 ($170,000) Jaguar, built by apprentices at the Midlands car factory, was a scale model of the real thing which could get up to speeds of 20 miles an hour. While William was able to turn the steering wheel, in reality his detective had full command. He stood nearby and operated a radio-control box which varied the car's speed and direction. All went well until the car failed to respond to the controls and the Jaguar careered into a garage door. William ended up in floods of tears, the car's wing was wrecked and the Jaguar has remained in the tack room next to the stables ever since.

These days the Princes are encouraged in more traditional country pursuits. They are familiar figures on the lanes around Highgrove when their groom, Marion Cox, takes their ponies for a morning trot. While William has won several rosettes at local gymkhanas where he is entered under Marion's name, there is a feeling locally that the Princes should enjoy more advanced schooling in equestrian skills. Certainly William has proceeded beyond the stage where his mother can easily walk along the meadow guiding his pony Trigger on a leading rein. Last Christmas he joined the Queen for a canter over the fields surrounding Sandringham,

Prince William on his pony Trigger and Prince Harry on Smokey are often seen in the lanes around Highgrove with their groom Marion Cox. While William has entered local gymkhanas, Harry is considered the better horseman.

surprising his grandmother with his sense of adventure. 'He trotted along so fast I could barely keep up,' the Queen cheerily told her guests.

Diana's antipathy towards riding means that while she can encourage her boys from the sidelines, she cannot lead by example. By contrast she has conveyed her enthusiasm for swimming to her children who are both able to swim unaided in the outdoor pool at Highgrove. Swimming is one of Diana's main forms of relaxation and on overseas tours she goes to elaborate lengths to ensure she gets her daily dip. 'I don't swim to exercise, but to relax,' she once told lifeguard Skip Grant. There is no exception to this at Highgrove and when the pool is undergoing annual maintenance she is happy to drive to a public pool in the nearby town of Cirencester. In winter the pool is covered by a see-through plastic bubble. Her usual routine starts at 7 o'clock when she slips out of her silk pyjamas, chooses her blue one-piece or pink bikini from the chest of drawers in her bathroom, and walks out through the french doors to the pool. Diana, who always wears a full-length white towelling robe here, has such a regular regime that the duty policeman knows to turn off the camera that monitors the pool. She dislikes the thought of constantly being on show.

The uniformed police take their security duties seriously. Before she goes swimming they carefully remove a 12-inch slab from a Cotswold stone wall which runs nearby. It gives them an uninterrupted view of the pool without being spotted. As they stand there, peeping at the Princess, they know that Diana swims for about thirty minutes before drying herself and going indoors for breakfast.

The royal couple eat in the dining room and, as at Kensington Palace, it is a light meal. She normally chooses between pink grapefruit, wheatgerm toast, Harvest Crunch cereal or Bemax while Charles picks Uncle Toby muesli, specially imported from Australia, or fresh fruit, Victoria plums being a favourite. Both drink scented Earl Grey tea with lemon on the side.

On Sunday mornings they like to linger over the newspapers. Charles takes the *Sunday Times* while other members of staff buy the tabloids.

'The garden is Prince Charles's pride and joy but holds little allure for the Princess.'

Diana reads them all. Normally if there is a derogatory article in one paper, the staff make excuses for its absence saying that it has not been delivered. Diana always knows the real reason and wheedles the offending journal from a member of staff. Charles's normal reaction to a negative Press is to raise his arms in horror and exclaim in strangled tones, 'Why do they do this to me? I can't understand it.' It is little wonder that the Prince is a caricaturist's dream.

Then the Prince dons his black gumboots, cords, sweater, gloves and flat cap, once worn by his father, and works off his aggression in the garden. He potters about from first light until the sun goes down and has perfected a technique where he can change in ten minutes before heading off in a helicopter for a royal engagement. While the garden is Charles's pride and joy, it holds little allure for the Princess. However, she has been enthused by the recent innovation of a rose garden. Earl Spencer has a formal rose garden at Althorp in which Diana used to wander around as a child, collecting petals to make into fragrant pot pourri. At Highgrove Charles is growing traditional, strongly scented roses which are an essential ingredient in making perfume.

He is keen to make his own brand of perfume oil and has recently enlisted the services of two experts, Rosemary Verey, the author of *The Fragrant Garden* who lives nearby, and Dr Peter Wilde whom he met at a Small Firms Merit Award prize-giving ceremony at Highgrove. Dr Wilde, a Yorkshireman who makes his own rose oil and soaps, was shown round the gardens by the Prince and he suggested that Charles could process his own plant oils.

His idea has taken hold and last April he began the experiment to extract fragrances from the roses and Greek 'datura' plants in his garden. Initially he wants to be able to produce enough oil for use in aromatherapy, a type of massage which uses essential oils to induce a sense of

Prince Charles and his gardener Dennis Brown discuss plans for the garden. The Prince is now considering making his own brand of Highgrove perfume as well as rose oils for aromatherapy.

well-being and relaxation. Diana, who has recently discovered the joys of this form of massage, is taking an active interest in the experiment.

Ultimately he would like to produce home-grown Highgrove perfume and oils to give to friends and family. This imaginative application of the fruits from their garden has gone even further as mentioned earlier for Prince Charles is exploring the possibility of using Highgrove rose oil as a component in the Holy Oil which will be used for his own Coronation. Dr Wilde observes, 'If the Prince does follow through this scheme to make his own Holy Oil it would be do-it-yourself on a truly majestic scale.'

There is a secret recipe for the oil with which the Archbishop of Canterbury anoints the monarch and his consort. At the Queen's Coronation in 1953 it was discovered that a precious phial of the oil, dating back to Queen Victoria's Coronation in 1837, had been broken. A London perfumier concocted another phial using the ancient recipe which is held by the Department of Muniments at Westminster Abbey.

The fact that the Prince is now actively pondering his accession not merely in general terms but down to the minutiæ of the origin of the oil to be used in the anointing ceremony at his Coronation indicates a profound change of thought. It is the first tangible evidence, albeit obscure, that the Queen and her successor may have laid secret plans to effect a suitable transition of office at some future point. The public are prepared. In poll after poll the indications are that the majority of the Queen's subjects would accept her abdication because they feel that the Prince of Wales is a worthy successor.

While this scheme to make rose oil has intriguing ramifications it must be approached in the context of Charles's use of Highgrove as a centre for experiment. It is part of his wider vision of producing, processing and marketing produce within the community, where the home is a viable economic centre.

His schemes are not always successful. For a time he equipped his dairy herd with bells hoping that the melodious sound would increase the milk yield. All it did was keep the neighbours awake at night. Eventually the bells were given away to charity. His attempts to market his own cheese through Marks and Spencer

Highgrove is almost self-sufficient, as numerous guests have discovered. When the Queen Mother and Ruth, Lady Fermoy spent one summer's day with the royal couple they enjoyed a picnic on the patio of cold sorrel soup as a starter, followed by chicken vol-au-vents, salad and fruit. Everything came from the garden, including the free-range hen. Only the white wine came from elsewhere.

When she is alone the Princess skips lunch, preferring to eat a packet of crisps or a bar of chocolate. Indeed, while she stops her children having too many sweets, she has no such compunction herself. When she goes for a drive she often stops at a store and picks up a packet of sweets to chew on the journey. Wise hosts cater

A face in the crowd – the Princess enjoys a few moments of anonymity as she mingles with the public at Badminton *(left)*. On a weekend visit to the Burghley Horse Trials *(below)* Diana, who likes to have her Christmas shopping finished by October, bought a pair of moccasin slippers.

stores failed as did an effort at harvesting the seeds of the wildflowers which grow along the driveway.

What is an undoubted triumph is the vegetable garden which now supplies the needs of his family and staff. It is a source of great pride, a satisfaction which Armand Hammer witnessed when he visited Highgrove one weekend. He says, 'When we were about to leave, Prince Charles suddenly disappeared and returned to present us with several boxes of the plump, sweet strawberries which he had picked himself as a present to us. I think his pleasure in those strawberries tells you all you need to know about him. He was more delighted to give us berries he had grown, and picked with his own hands, than if they had been jewels from the family vault.'

for her needs. During a visit to a friend's Scottish estate she was pleasantly surprised when she was presented with a box of her favourite Charbonnel et Walker *boîte blanche* chocolates as she was being formally introduced to the other guests. It was explained that confidential inquiries had been made among her circle of friends to discover her secret passion.

At lunchtime Charles has a similarly frugal appetite. Even after a hard morning working in the garden, he is happy with a sandwich before going off to play polo at Windsor or Cirencester.

One of the original reasons for buying Highgrove was its proximity to the Beaufort and Bicester hunts. These days, however, he spends more time with the more distant and fashionable Belvoir and Quorn hunts, stabling his horses at the Household Cavalry's quarters in Melton Mowbray, Leicestershire, so that they are convenient for the meet.

While Charles is passionate about hunting – he once refused to speak to a servant for a week when he tactlessly remarked that Oscar Wilde was right when he said that fox hunting was 'the pursuit of the inedible by the unspeakable' – Diana is entirely uninterested. She rarely accompanies him and only went to watch him at one meet in Leicestershire so that she could visit her sister Sarah.

If it is a fine day she will take the boys to watch papa play polo at the Guards' Polo Club at Windsor, presenting the prizes if it is in honour of one of her favourite charities like Birthright. However polo is hardly the most riveting of spectator sports. When it is coupled with the constant attentions of photographers it can feel more like a public engagement than an afternoon at leisure.

The boys entertain themselves by feeding the polo ponies sugar lumps or playing doctors and patients in the St John's ambulance which stands by in readiness. When the boys get bored, which is frequently, Diana either takes them back to Highgrove or to Kensington Palace so that they are ready for school the following day.

In the winter when Charles is away at the hunt, Diana entertains the boys by taking them for a drive round the grounds or helping them with their homework. Last year she took William for skiing lessons at a nearby dry ski

Charles and Diana take pride in the fact that all the produce at Highgrove is home grown. Punnets of strawberries are often given to guests as 'farewell gifts'. The Prince has encouraged his children to take up gardening by giving them their own small plots to cultivate.

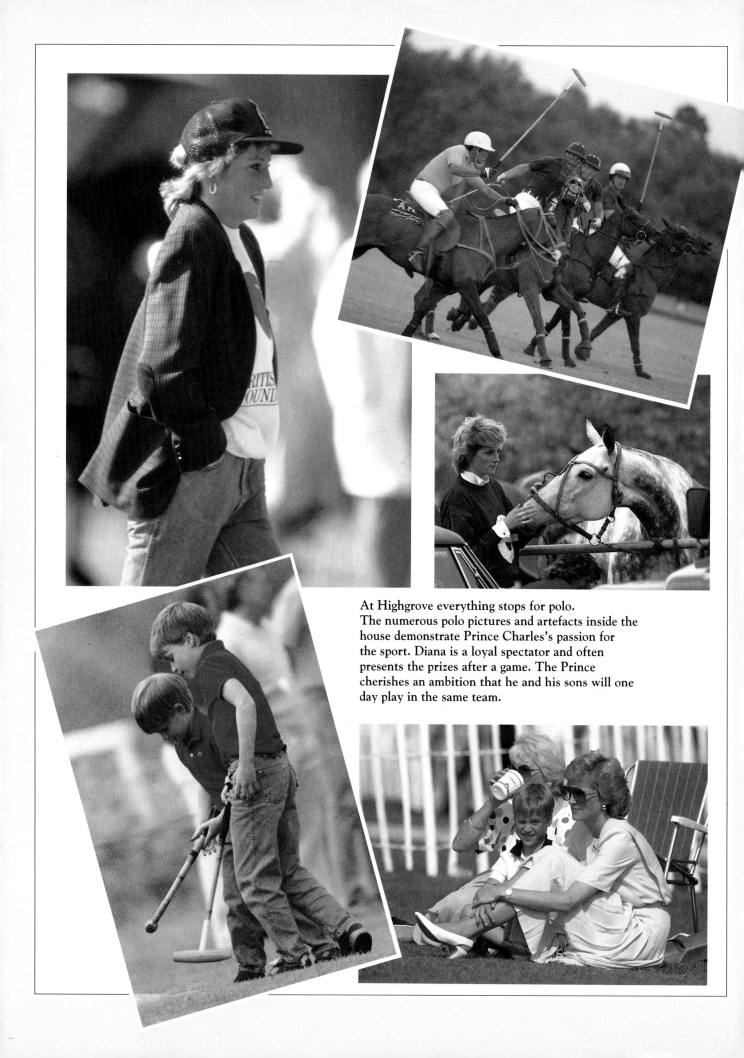

At Highgrove everything stops for polo.
The numerous polo pictures and artefacts inside the
house demonstrate Prince Charles's passion for
the sport. Diana is a loyal spectator and often
presents the prizes after a game. The Prince
cherishes an ambition that he and his sons will one
day play in the same team.

school. 'He loved it,' she proudly announced although he has yet to make the transition to the real thing.

If the boys are out riding with Marion Cox, Diana slips out for a couple of hours shopping, a scarf or baseball hat disguising her appearance and her detective Ken Wharfe by her side. She sometimes pops in to the Gateway supermarket in Tetbury to buy frozen hamburgers for the boys' supper and occasionally drops in to Phillips the baker to buy their special pink elephant and yellow lovebird meringues as a teatime indulgence.

Since the Wales moved to Highgrove, Tetbury has become a thriving tourist centre and several of the shops, including the chemist, dry cleaner and Paintons the greengrocer (where Diana orders her freesias), have sprouted distinctive Prince of Wales feathers over their doors, denoting their elevation to 'By Appointment' status. The Wales try to live up to their billing as the local 'squires' by donating to local charities – Diana gave £1,000 ($1,700) to the town playgroup while every year Charles invites local pensioners and farmers to tour the gardens and sends excess produce from the vegetable garden to local hospitals and old people's homes.

Occasionally Diana heads further afield. In the elegant Regency town of Bath she may visit the Body Shop to replenish her cosmetics or the Gap store to buy tee-shirts, shorts and swimming trunks for her boys. However, she prefers Cirencester where it is easier to park her open-top Jaguar XJS and she is frequently spotted heading into the General Trading Company – a branch of the London store which held her wedding list – to buy presents. Just down the High Street is the Surprises gift store which stocks greetings and birthday cards for the Princess. Last year she sent friends an amusing Christmas card featuring the Queen on the front moaning about having to endure visits from relatives. 'And like you, one will be very pleased when they all go home,' ran the legend. Owner Penny Hall says, 'We have got used to her coming in. She is terribly nice. Our customers don't make a great fuss. It's all very low key.'

Another customer is the Princess Royal who visits the gift shop rather more frequently than

The Princess, casually dressed in shorts and tee-shirt, often drives to Cirencester for a morning's shopping. At the local record store Diana, who prefers classical music, once jokingly asked for the latest offering by the crooner Val Doonican.

she sees her brother and sister-in-law – even though she lives nearby at Gatcombe Park. However her children, Zara and Peter, accompanied by their nanny, do visit William and Harry and mayhem regularly results. 'When Zara and William get together they are a precocious pair of rascals,' says one member of staff. In the course of one afternoon the young scamps managed to draw faces in felt pen on all the white paintwork in the nursery, giving staff the unenviable task of cleaning it all off.

Even Princess Anne has difficulty controlling the royal tearaways. She looked after the foursome for one weekend at Windsor Castle when Diana and Charles were on an overseas tour. She entertained them by taking them out kite flying. Zara and William soon tired of that and spent the rest of the afternoon rolling down a carefully manicured lawn, destroying hours of work by the royal gardeners.

The youngsters play cricket although William manages to ignore the rules no matter how carefully Peter Phillips explains them. He is less concerned about the niceties of his stance at the crease than in hitting the ball as far as he can.

However, the favoured pastime when the Princes' cousins visit Highgrove is to 'help' with the farming when William loves to steer the tractor. An hour's riding around the estate, feeding the animals (the boys have a pet rabbit and a gerbil), hunting for eggs laid in the bales of hay in the stables or swimming in the pool soon takes up an afternoon.

William already has the countryman's robust attitude towards farm stock. He once provoked a shriek of alarm from Diana when he proudly brought the corpse of a decaying rabbit into the house. He had seen the gardeners bury the creature and then promptly dug it up when they had gone.

Harry has inherited his father's more sensitive approach which Prince Charles recognizes. 'He's the quieter of the two,' he says, and he is frequently seen pointing out the flowers to his youngest son as they wander, hand in hand,

Prince Harry has inherited his father's sensitive temperament and Prince Charles is often seen pointing out the flowers to his son in the garden.

around the country garden. 'Be gentle to flowers, they will never hurt you,' is a rule Harry learned at an early age. That does not apply to animals, as the Prince learned to his cost. Harry was terrified when he was attacked in the courtyard one morning by a rogue cockerel which lived in the stables. He was in such a state of shock that the aggressive bird had its neck wrung shortly afterwards.

Even though he is a working farmer Charles does have a soft spot for animals. The Prince encouraged a pair of barn owls to nest in the trees and turns a blind eye to the fox that roots around in the cottage garden. He once employed a mole catcher to rid his daisy-covered lawn of the pests. However, he was rather too successful. After a day's work he displayed seventeen moles which had fallen victim to his traps. The Prince congratulated him on his efforts adding, 'Don't kill them all will you?'

He showed no such leniency when he decided to 'dock' or cut short the tail of Tigger, the Jack Russell terrier given as a wedding present by his gardening advisor Lady Salisbury. Diana disagreed, arguing that the operation, performed under a local anaesthetic by the vet, was cruel and pointless. The altercation symbolizes the differences between them.

Charles is the countryman who accepts traditional lore, abides by the rhythm of the seasons and enjoys conventional pursuits like fox hunting, riding, polo and gardening. Diana is a young woman who prefers the pleasures of the metropolis and fills the long days in the country by swimming, going for long walks with her Sony Walkman stereo clamped to her head, reading a book in the shade of an ornamental tree or garden seat and chatting to her friends on the telephone. Even her ambition to build a tennis court was thwarted. Unfortunately it was too near the compost heap and the odour stopped play. It is now a car park. But she occasionally manages a game at the nearby Hare and Hounds Hotel at Westonbirt.

The friends she sees in London rarely come to Highgrove. It is regarded as 'off limits', a strict sanctuary where the majority of the visitors are from their own families or are European royals. The names in the visitors' book reflect this. The Queen Mother, ex-King Constantine and Queen

Diana at a Sunday polo match.

Anne-Marie of Greece, the most frequent guests, the Princess Royal (only two visits), Princess Margaret's former husband, Lord Snowdon, Earl Spencer as well as an Arab Prince who left a picture of himself in a huge solid-gold frame when he left. Near neighbours like Andrew and Camilla Parker-Bowles and Lady Salisbury or William's godfather, Sir Laurens van der Post and his analyst wife, Ingaret, are invited from time to time.

While Diana is mistress of the house, she must still observe the Court civilities, curtsying to the Queen Mother and King Constantine when she greets them on the gravel drive. However royal rituals are soon dispensed with, the Prince usually taking his visitors on a tour of the gardens and his farm at Broadfield where he keeps dairy cows and sheep. Earl Spencer got the full treatment when he made a weekend visit, although it was William who was his energetic host. When they reached a five-bar gate William said sternly, 'I can't open it, Grandpa, you've got to climb it, otherwise the animals will get out.' Meekly the 8th Earl did as he was bid, observing afterwards, 'William lectures me.'

A tour of the farm to admire Charles's organic methods or a stroll round the garden imbibing the scents from traditional flowers like delphiniums, lavender and marigolds works up an appetite for dinner. If their guests are of sufficient station the royal butler Harold Brown will drive down from Kensington Palace to organize the event. Discerning visitors can tell if they are receiving first- or second-class hospitality by the cutlery on the table. The George III silver, kept in the dining room, is only brought out for very special guests although everyone dines off their green and gold Spode dinner service.

Even though formality is kept to a minimum, black tie is still *de rigueur* at dinner. These days the menus are determined by the rhythm of the seasons as much as the wishes of the hostess. If Charles has had a successful fishing trip on the River Dee at Balmoral, guests can expect salmon mousse as a starter and a main course of trout with almonds. Or dinner could have a distinctly Latin flavour. Last year his garden produced so much basil that his temporary Italian chef turned it into pesto sauce to serve with tomatoes and pasta.

While the royal couple are virtually teetotal, in the summer they do make an exception, sipping Pimm's fruit cup – 'so refreshing' says Charles – on the patio as they watch the sun go down. Charles's only other concession to alcohol is during the hunting season. He pours a lethal mixture of gin and cherry brandy into his hip flask before he leaves and on his return makes his own martini from a tray of drinks especially laid out for him in Diana's study.

Normally a bottle of white wine, usually German, will suffice for a royal dinner party, the company retiring to the drawing room for coffee afterwards. If they are on their own they regularly have a light three-course meal on a tray, decorated with a single pink rose, and sit and watch the television in Diana's study. She enjoys soaps like 'EastEnders' – in her bathroom is an EastEnders mug for her toothbrushes – and finds the witty caricatures of the royal family which feature in the satirical puppet show, 'Spitting Image' a 'scream'.

At Highgrove the royal couple rarely stay up later than 11 o'clock, Charles often falling asleep over the papers in his study or slumped in his chair in front of the television. When they have retired, nothing disturbs the repose of Diana's weekend retreat save the slow tread of the duty policeman as he makes his silent rounds keeping a sharp eye for intruders, especially of the feline kind.

CHAPTER FOUR

Diana after Dark

She sparkles at first nights, she dazzles at film premières and she shines at dinner parties. When the lights go down the Princess of Wales really brightens up. One minute she behaves like a star-struck teenager, the next her witty sophisticated fashions invest an evening with excitement.

Nervy and highly strung, she is above all a performer who thrills to the applause of the crowd and revels in the surprise of a dramatic entrance. 'You're really enjoying all this attention,' one dancing partner told her as they waltzed together, watched by everyone present at a charity ball. While she does not like to be reminded of it, the Princess thoroughly enjoys being the star of the royal roadshow. Occasions such as her sensational stage appearance with Wayne Sleep at Covent Garden in December 1985 and, in the same year, the dance routine performed in front of the Reagans at the White House with *Saturday Night Fever* star John Travolta underline how she loves the spotlight.

Perhaps it is as well that she never realized her ambition to become a prima ballerina. Instead, she has succeeded in making the world her stage and her role as the Princess of Wales a constantly startling spectacle.

Theatre and costume are at the heart of the pomp and circumstance that is the Crown.

Diana dazzles after dark, adding glitter to the starriest occasion. She had a special reason to smile following the première of *Dangerous Liaisons*. The film's star, John Malkovich, asked Diana if breakfasts at Kensington Palace resembled the lustful antics of the French aristocracy portrayed in the movie. 'No,' she replied, 'but it beats reading the papers.'

Indeed royalty is the original street theatre, the brilliant processions and stunning pageants the lifeblood of monarchy. Princess Diana is following in the footsteps of Edward VII, Queen Mary, the Queen Mother, Princess Margaret and Lord Snowdon as a member of the royal family who takes pleasure in the theatricality of royalty. By contrast the Queen, Prince Philip and Prince Charles are from the Prince Albert school of monarchy, content to play their parts but without the enthusiasm of the born performer.

Even though she is a leading member of the world's longest-established troupe, surprisingly Diana still has first-night nerves. The girl who never missed an episode of the glitzy soap opera 'Dynasty' feels those fluttering butterflies when she meets stars like Elizabeth Taylor, Charles Dance and Nigel Havers. Actress Marisa Berenson, once voted the world's most beautiful woman, observed her at the Cannes Film Festival and feels there is still something of the awed teenager about Diana. She says, 'The Princess has the reputation in Hollywood of being rather star struck.'

As she carefully dressed for the world première of the James Bond movie *Octopussy*, she confessed that she was 'so excited' at the prospect of meeting Roger Moore, the suave actor who plays 007. When she arrived she outgunned the Bond girls in her silver, off-the-shoulder evening gown. The effect was deliberate. As a consummate performer, the Princess expends much thought and energy into making an impact while deftly complimenting her hosts in an outfit which reflects the occasion. Her achievement has been to combine the panache of the

'Her look, which is so effective, is the result of total grooming.'

Regency dandy with the modesty of the royal Court, modish extravagance within the bounds of good taste and proper form.

For example when she appeared at the first night of *Steel Magnolias*, she and her designer Catherine Walker had decided to embroider passion flowers into her gown. Again it was her idea to ask Gieves and Hawkes, the By Appointment tailors, to make her an officer's mess jacket when she dined with the Royal Hampshire Regiment, of which she is Colonel-in-Chief.

In her striking mess jacket of the Royal Hampshire Regiment, Princess Diana makes her own fashion statement while complimenting her military hosts.

However, a princess has more than mere film-star appeal and Diana has taken note of the mistakes she made during the 1980s when her attempts at a Hollywood look provoked numerous 'Dynasty Di' headlines. Her look, which seems so effortless, is the result of total grooming. Beauty is not just in the eye of the beholder: it must also be in the mind of the beholden. Everything from her fitness routine and her astrological counselling down to her hairdressing and make-up prepare the Princess to face the world with serenity and confidence. The days when she thought, 'Oh gosh, help, panic' before she undertook a run-of-the-mill royal engagement are largely behind her.

Before she attends a banquet or first night, the Princess undergoes a beauty routine which combines attention to detail with the tricks of the cosmetic trade. It is a procedure which gives her time to gather her energy for the evening ahead. Normally her hairdresser Richard Dalton is, of course, on hand and sometimes if it is the night of a 'big dressing' when all the royal ladies wear their tiaras, make-up artist Barbara Daly is present. Daly, who did the make-up for the Princess's wedding, has shown her how to make the best use of her cosmetics, utilizing full daylight where possible and using sable brushes to soften the effect of the powders. One of her first decisions was to throw away Diana's pink blusher, which accentuated her high colour, and convert to a russet shade.

While Barbara Daly has been her make-up guru, the Princess is not averse to stealing ideas from Hollywood. She has always been a fan of Elizabeth Taylor and was thrilled to meet her in 1982 when she starred in *The Little Foxes* in the West End. During the encounter Diana closely studied Taylor's almost mesmeric eyes and shortly afterwards started to use stronger eyeliner on the upper lids to give her eyes better definition, as well as applying brilliant blue on the inner rim of the lower eyelids.

Barbara Daly says, 'She has now found her make-up style which is terribly simple but looks

Opposite: **The Princess puts much time and energy into making an impact. She looked every inch the Regency dandy in this Rifat Ozbek outfit when she arrived at a fashion show in Madrid.**

A few of Diana's make-up ideas have come from Hollywood. The brilliant blue eyeliner she uses on her upper and lower lids is a technique she learned from Elizabeth Taylor.

fabulous. The Princess has such good skin that she doesn't need foundation and she only uses a tiny touch of blusher to add shape to her cheeks. She prefers brown and taupe eyeshadows which she knows look best when applied slightly darker at the edge of the eyes.' At the same time heavy lipstick is not her style. Instead she uses a light lip gloss at night to go with whatever outfit she chooses.

But as Barbara Daly points out, 'Really beauty has nothing to do with what you put on the outside. The Princess is a lovely person and it shines through. I've seen her without a trace of cosmetics and she is still lovely.'

This natural complexion still needs a little artificial assistance to keep it in tone. For the last six years Diana has visited beauty expert Janet Filderman who gives her a gentle facial massage with the special cleansers and creams she has developed. The Princess's beauty therapist, a diffident Yorkshirewoman, has a direct, straight-forward approach to skin care which has enabled her to build a portfolio of famous names including the Duchess of Kent and actress Maryam D'Abo. In her salon near Harley Street are framed Christmas cards from the Princess in appreciation of her efforts during the year.

Janet, who uses the same techniques for Diana as her other clients, says, 'My beauty philosophy is quite simple – do not overload the skin. It is an animate protective organ which does react with what is put on it. My special technique is to vacuum suction to cleanse the skin. I use a small electric motor attached to a glass phial which gently "Hoovers" the skin to remove dirt and unblock the pores. Then I use massage which presses blood out of the facial muscles and is replaced instantly with fresh oxygenated blood. The combined operation of vacuum suction and massage with creams gets rid of stale impurities and tones up the face. The result is both relaxation and radiance.'

The Princess also puts her health in the hands of another therapist from Yorkshire. Former miner Joseph Corvo has been treating Diana, her grandmother, Ruth, Lady Fermoy and her step-grandmother, the novelist Barbara Cartland for decades. He uses the unconventional technique of zone therapy to induce a sense of well-being in the Princess. The Duchess of York, who regularly visits his modest apartment in Marylebone, central London, calls him 'Joe the Toe' because of the way he massages the feet to diagnose the body's general ills. His technique is nothing new – zone therapy was first practised by the Chinese. It works by identifying and massaging fifteen key pressure points which correspond to specific parts of the body. So massaging the back of the jaw improves the sex drive, the tip of the nose is linked to the liver and stomach while rubbing the forehead helps spark the brain into action.

The theory is that the body is an electro-magnetic field and that various nerves connected

Total grooming is the secret of Diana's success. From her sleek cropped hair to the decision to choose one red and one black glove for this **Murray Arbeid dress, the Princess has carefully thought through her style.**

to our internal organs can become clogged and choked by poor diet or lack of exercise. Massaging these vital areas helps to tone the muscles, stimulate the glands and put a glow back into your cheeks. Everything from migraine, overweight, constipation and infertility can be helped by undergoing a regular 15-minute massage which gradually disperses the toxins in the body.

The end result of all this attention is a young woman who, as hatmaker John Boyd observes, 'just glows in the evening'. Before she goes out at night, the finishing touches are regularly inspired by Richard Dalton. He suggested she attend a film première wearing one black and one red glove to complement her Murray Arbeid dress and convinced her that she should wear a chiffon scarf slung round her neck as a fitting compliment to Grace Kelly when she attended the Cannes Film Festival in 1987.

His most dramatic influences have been reserved for her jewellery. The outsize Mary Queen of Scots cross, borrowed from Wartskis the jewellers, was one idea, the rope of fake pearls she wore down her uncovered back was another. As a metropolitan royal, the attitude of the Princess of Wales towards her jewellery harks back to another era. Fake or real, the Princess does not mind if it adds to the total look. On one occasion she was on her way to London Heathrow airport for a royal tour when she asked the entourage to make a brief diversion. She dashed into the Fulham Road shop of Butler and Wilson, famous for fake rocks, and bought a pair of red and black earrings.

Unlike the Queen who has hardly altered a setting since she ascended the throne, the Princess likes ringing the changes. For example she turned a diamond and sapphire watch, a wedding gift from the Saudi Arabian royal family, into a striking headband for her meeting with the late Emperor Hirohito of Japan. Perhaps her most daring innovation was in agreeing to Richard Dalton's suggestion to wear Queen Mary's emerald Art Deco necklace as a headband at a dinner dance in Australia. As Prince Charles whirled her around the dance floor, Diana positively purred with delight at the commotion she caused among the watching media.

All this was but a foretaste of the explosion of astonishment which greeted her appearance on stage with the dancer, Wayne Sleep. He recalls, 'There was a gasp so huge that it hit the stage like a rocket, then it burst into an incredible roar of near-disbelief. I was frightened the Princess would be put off by the reaction, but she behaved as if she'd been dancing for an audience all her life.' For when Diana goes out at night

The Princess wears jewellery with daring and adventure. She once wore Queen Mary's emerald necklace, which the Queen gave Diana as a wedding present, as a headband.

she is not merely content to look sensational, she loves to dance the night away. Their three-minute performance of the Billy Joel hit, 'Uptown Girl', had been secretly rehearsed at Kensington Palace as a surprise for Prince Charles. When the routine ended, Diana curtsied to the Royal Box as if she was a member of the cast.

What neither Wayne Sleep nor any of the audience were aware of was the special significance the Royal Opera House holds for the Prince and Princess. An evening at this Covent Garden venue was the setting for their first-ever date together. Normally when Prince Charles takes a group of friends to the Royal Box, the number in the party is known well in advance. However in November 1979, almost nine months before the world first spotted them on the banks of the River Dee in Balmoral, the Prince sent a hasty handwritten memo to Captain Ward, then a member of the Household, informing him that an 'additional guest, Lady Diana Spencer (Ruth Fermoy's granddaughter)', would be joining him for the evening.

The name was unknown to the Prince's staff until that time. Indeed the fact that Charles had to identify her by referring to the Queen Mother's lady-in-waiting, underlines her anonymity. Certainly Diana was impressed by the royal hospitality on offer on that historic evening. At the rear of the Royal Box is a private dining room which the Prince's staff spend two hours preparing before the royal party arrive. The table is laid with solid-silver cutlery, Spode china and Brierley crystal. Indeed when Alan Fisher was the Wales' butler he even brought candelabra to add to the sense of occasion as the party enjoyed a light supper.

While Charles visits Covent Garden for the opera with Sir Laurens van der Post, Lady 'Kanga' Tryon and Lady Susan Hussey, the Queen's lady-in-waiting, as regular guests in his party, the Princess prefers the ballet. For Diana ballet is far more than mere exercise to stay in shape, it is a way of life. As patron of the London City and English National Ballet companies she attends as many of their opening nights as she can.

These gala evenings are the events she relishes most in her royal calendar. The chance to meet and work with top dancers is an ambition she has held since childhood. Her former nurserymaid Inge Crane saw Diana take her first ballet lesson as an enthusiastic five-year-old. She recalls, 'I used to watch Diana and her sisters Sarah and Jane dancing around the nursery. Diana was lost in a fantasy world as she danced dressed up in her mother's old clothes. She tried to copy the older girls but even then I could see that she had tremendous natural ability.'

At West Heath School in Kent, Diana made sure her name was top of the list for ballet trips to the Coliseum or Sadler's Wells. She saw *Swan Lake* four times and wept when she watched *Sleeping Beauty*.

While she won the school prize for dance and took her first job as a teacher at Madame Vacani's famous ballet school, she realized that she was too tall to make the grade. Now her love is channelled into regular ballet workouts with fellow dancers. Instructor Deirdra Lovell says, 'She begins with a technical warm-up to loosen up the head and torso. Then she concentrates on fluid movements, finally creating her routine. The music is a vital element.'

Indeed during the build-up to the royal wedding in 1981 the Princess of Wales found solace in her love of dancing. It was her way of coping with the extraordinary pressure she came under as her temporary home at Buckingham Palace faced a daily siege. She invited the West Heath School pianist, the late Lilian Snipp, and Wendy Mitchell, her dance teacher, to the Palace to give her private lessons. For forty minutes Diana, dressed in a black leotard, went through a routine that combined ballet with tap dancing.

During those momentous days Lily Snipp kept a diary, hitherto unpublished, which gives a first-hand feeling of the misgivings felt by Lady Diana Spencer as the wedding day approached. She lost so much weight that the dress, made by David and Elizabeth Emanuel, had to be taken in by four inches and she confided that she felt her freedom was slipping away.

The first entry in Miss Snipp's diary, on Friday, 5 June 1981, recorded details of Diana's first lesson. She wrote: 'To Buckingham Palace to play for Lady Diana. We all worked hard at the lesson, no time wasted. When the lesson was over Lady Diana, with her tongue in her cheek said, "I suppose Miss Snipp will now go direct to Fleet Street." She has a good sense of humour – she will need it in the years to come.'

Her second lesson a week later saw a less energetic pupil. Miss Snipp wrote: 'Saudi Arabians were visiting – glimpse of the State Banqueting Hall being dismantled after the previous night's party. Lady Diana was tired after the long party – it must have been very hard

Diana attends a performance of the Bolshoi Ballet at the Royal Opera House. The ballet holds special significance for Diana. On her first evening out with Prince Charles, he treated her to the Royal Box at Covent Garden.

work talking to so many people some unable to speak English. Today was the first day she rehearsed getting into the Glass Coach with her wedding gown on. Lady Diana enjoyed her dancing lesson and looked refreshed afterwards having left her other cares behind for an hour.'

Two weeks later Diana enjoyed her first audience – ten of the Queen's corgis stared at her through the window as she danced in the Music Room. But Diana was upset that her new tap shoes had scored the splendid wooden floor designed by John Nash in 1830. Miss Snipp and Wendy Vickers were taken by the Master of the Royal Household to another room where they were informed 'the floor doesn't matter'. To their surprise and amusement they discovered it was the Queen's Throne Room and numerous Palace workmen manhandled a grand piano into the room for the lesson.

Perhaps the most poignant lesson, the last for the time being, was held a few days before the wedding. Diana's thoughts were on the profound changes ahead. Miss Snipp noted: 'Lady Diana rather tired – too many late nights. I delivered silver salt cellars, a present from West Heath School, very beautiful and much admired. Lady Diana counting how many days of freedom are left to her. Rather sad. Masses of people outside of Palace. We hope to resume lessons in October. Lady Diana said, "In twelve days time I shall no longer be me."'

Shortly after her honeymoon Diana became pregnant and dancing lessons were not resumed until after Prince William's birth. Miss Snipp immediately noted the changes in the Princess when, on 11 November 1982, she arrived at Buckingham Palace for a lesson.

Miss Snipp wrote: 'We curtsied and Diana came and shook hands with us and said how pleased she was to see us again. Diana looked very beautiful and very *thin*. (Her doctor wants her to increase her weight – she has no appetite.) I enquired after Prince William – he slept 13 hours last night! She said that she and Charles are besotted parents! And their son is wonderful. The Master of the Queen's Household came to make sure the floor was alright (hardboard floor laid down). Both Diana and Wendy worked very hard – the first exercise Diana has done since the birth.'

A week later Miss Snipp visited Kensington Palace and recorded her impressions on what was to be her first and last trip to Diana's new home. She wrote: 'Kens Palace consists of several homes like a village. Entered hall door – greeted by Alan [Fisher]. Beautiful painting of Diana hanging on wall of staircase – taken to drawing room where the carpet has been rolled up ready for Diana to dance on polished wooden floor. New Broadwood piano covered in portraits of the royals, books and beautiful lamp. Had to ask for books and portraits to be moved so as to find music rack. Diana greeted us both with a lovely smile, shook hands and hoped we didn't mind the extended journey! Prince Andrew stood outside looking up to our window. A lovely smile from him – Diana danced for one hour and looks far more relaxed today.'

While that was the last lesson from the team from her old school Diana continued to take lessons in the privacy of the west London studio of former ballet star Merle Park. However her love of dance is not confined to special stage shows or the privacy of the rehearsal room as we have seen.

This enthusiasm is not shared by Prince Charles. At official balls protocol demands that he and Diana are the first couple to dance. Invariably they are watched by fellow partygoers and photographers. It is a chore he likes to waltz through as quickly as possible. As he says, 'I assure you it makes the heart sink to have to make an awful exhibition of ourselves.'

Even when the cameramen are excluded, the Prince prefers conversation to creative expression on the dance floor. At the party to celebrate the Duke and Duchess of York's wedding held at Claridges, Charles stayed on the sidelines while Diana spent her evening dancing with a number of partners.

On other occasions Prince Charles leaves for home on his own while Diana stays behind because she is enjoying herself so much. At one party she was doing a frenetic whirlwind dance to Diana Ross's hit song, 'Chain Reaction'. 'She looked a dervish,' said one partygoer. 'I was astonished by her sense of rhythm.'

At another charity ball organized by Bruce Oldfield, a friend and a favourite designer, the

While Diana loves dancing the night away, it makes Charles's heart sink. At the White House banquet Nancy Reagan ensured that the Princess danced with actor John Travolta. True to form, Charles was more engrossed by Nancy Reagan's conversation than watching Diana's fancy footwork. He was missing too when singer Neil Diamond enjoyed a cheerful waltz with Diana.

royal Cinderella was scheduled to leave before midnight because, said her courtiers, she had a busy timetable of engagements the following day. Instead, she loved the music so much, and the company of French pop composer Jean Michel Jarre, that she stayed on. At one o'clock when Kid Creole and the Coconuts stopped playing the Princess walked over to the American singer and asked him to continue. 'I could keep dancing all night,' she told him. 'You see I get so few chances to go out dancing and there's nothing I love more.'

Even when she manages to enjoy herself, the Princess faces an additional problem. Her status means that many men are understandably hesitant about asking her to dance. Her predicament was observed by disc jockey Mike Read at a charity bash at London's Royal Albert Hall where she stood on the edge of the dance floor making polite conversation. He avoided the glares of her bodyguards and asked her to dance. 'It's nice that you can just walk up and ask her to dance. We sort of jigged about a bit – there wasn't really much room. In that situation the thing that occurs to you most is, "Is she thinking I'm a complete idiot?"'

It is not just Diana's position which leaves her sitting on the sidelines. At private parties the Princess, who frequently goes on her own, ends up as a wallflower because of the unspoken fear that her partners could feature prominently in the gossip columns. Brewery heir Peter Greenall was one innocent victim when he took her dancing to the Casa Antica disco in Klosters. Much was made of Charles's absence although the fact that Greenall was one of a large party which included five Swiss and Scotland Yard bodyguards was largely ignored.

On another occasion photographers camped outside the front door of financier Charles Carter for days. He had danced with the Princess of Wales at the Duchess of York's pre-wedding party at the Guards' Polo Club.

Party hosts who invite the Princess take extra care to ensure that she has a good time away from prying eyes. When Diana's friend Julia Samuel celebrated her thirtieth birthday by throwing a party at her Berkshire home the Princess was one of the hundreds of guests who enjoyed themselves into the early hours. Even

Early in her royal career Diana was often too exhausted to go out at night. Now she regularly goes out with a crowd of friends for dinner or to see a film.

though fireworks and the legendary Procol Harum were part of the noisy late-night entertainment, not a whisper about the Princess's presence reached the world outside.

Julia and her husband Michael were not so fortunate when they accompanied the Princess and Captain David Waterhouse to her local Odeon cinema on Kensington High Street. As they emerged from a screening of the Dustin Hoffman movie *Rain Man*, a photographer emerged from the shadows to snap Diana when

'When she goes out at night she can never be totally secure or private.'

she gave the Life Guards officer a friendly good-night kiss.

Normally Diana has more problems with usherettes who ask for her autograph but the incident highlights the flip side of Diana's life. When she goes out at night she can never feel totally secure or private. She is a lifetime prisoner of her position, a feeling of claustrophobia which occasionally spills over into tears of frustration. One late-night incident triggered a bout of uncharacteristic self-pity. Once again it was David Waterhouse who was the focus of attention when he and Diana, she dressed in satin trousers and a bomber jacket, emerged from the mews home of their mutual friend Kate Menzies. She jokingly tried to put a balloon over the exhaust of Waterhouse's Audi car. As they fooled around, freelance photographer Jason Fraser snapped the scene. The Princess, realizing the repercussions, pleaded with him to hand over his film. 'I've been working hard all week. Katie fixed up a nice evening for me. She laid this whole thing on. It's very sweet and it's the only time I've been out all week. I've got so few friends left and this will only make things worse for me,' she told Fraser.

The fact that Diana leads a very separate existence from her husband will always leave her open to this kind of incident, especially as many of her circle of friends have rarely met the Prince. While Diana did exaggerate the effect on her friends, it does create a climate of suspicion and anxiety. Many in her circle worry that a word or an action out of place could place a relationship in jeopardy. 'We are a new breed of Trappist monks. Silence is our vocation,' says one friend.

At the same time Diana's sense of vulnerability is heightened because she knows that, from time to time, she will be followed by a paparazzi photographer as she and her police escort drive through the West End. Indeed such are the rich pickings of pursuing the Princess that one enterprising cameraman hired a Formula Three racing driver in order to keep Diana in his sights. It is a headache for Diana's minders who feel that the antics of these freelance photographers hinder their primary role of personal protection.

The Princess tries not to allow these hazards to curtail her enjoyment of a private evening out. The Princess in her Jaguar XJS, followed by a police back-up Rover car, is a frequent visitor to theatreland where she likes to keep abreast of the latest shows. 'I always try and see everything,' she says. The long-running *Phantom of the Opera* has been graced by her presence at least three times.

When she went to the première of the comedy movie, *When Harry Met Sally*, she enjoyed it so much that she asked the film's star Meg Ryan to send her a video so that she could see it again in the privacy of Kensington Palace.

Her efforts to embrace a normal lifestyle do produce unexpected drawbacks. There were harsh words muttered in the front stalls when Diana arrived late and unannounced to see Andrew Lloyd Webber's *Aspects of Love*.

Diana loves to see the latest West End shows, wearing slinky outfits that would cause a sensation at a public engagement.

Unfortunately someone was already occupying her seat and the man, not recognizing the Princess in the gloom, refused to move until the house manager intervened. On another occasion it was claimed that she sent her bodyguard to haggle with ticket touts so that she could see the sell-out show, *Les Misérables*.

Over-zealous bodyguards caused another scene when she was driving through the West End to see the comedian Rowan Atkinson in his one-man show. As she crawled along Shaftesbury Avenue the lights turned red and her police back-up car had to jump the lights to keep behind her. As a result the police car blocked the rest of the traffic. An irate taxi driver shouted a stream of abuse at the policeman, not realizing that the Princess could hear. When she arrived at the theatre she told the police driver with a smile, 'I think I understand what the taxi driver was getting at.'

At the end of a show she returns to the home of one of her friends for a light supper, even loaning them her chef to make the preparations so that they can join her at the theatre or cinema. Like Princess Margaret, Diana likes to mix with the stars after the show. She waited until *Phantom* star Michael Crawford took off his make-up to join him for dinner while she has been out on the town with Wayne Sleep and choreographer Gillian Lynne.

In the evening when Diana entertains at Kensington Palace, she often has a serious purpose in mind. With her growing portfolio of patronages, she frequently employs the State Apartments as the grand setting for cocktail parties.

During one reception in aid of the British fashion industry she confessed that she was feeling close to tears. It was just days after the Klosters tragedy but she soldiered on regardless. She had much more fun when the cream of the pop industry, including Kate Bush and ex-Beatle George Harrison, were invited to Kensington Palace as a thank-you for their efforts on behalf of the Prince's Trust. The Princess was delighted when both Elton John and Labi Siffre took turns on the piano.

Dinner parties at the Court of Diana and Charles often have an earnest motive, usually to meet the leaders of Britain's science, arts and

The Princess of Wales enjoys entertaining the stars to a late supper after the performance.

political communities. Prime Minister Margaret Thatcher, the Labour leader Neil Kinnock, the film-maker Sir Richard Attenborough, opera singer Placido Domingo, and rock star Bob Geldof have all enjoyed the Wales' hospitality. Aled Jones, the brilliant young Welsh treble, was delighted to be asked to the Palace.

Dress is formal but the atmosphere is relaxed. Diana will often bring in the children to say goodnight. Indeed when William and Harry were babies she loved to show the infants off to her friends. The routine is similar to lunch. Drinks are served in the drawing room before the company, between twelve and sixteen strong, enter the dining room for dinner at 8.30 p.m.

The table setting, as at Highgrove, of George III silver, Brierley crystal and green and gold

Spode china is often more elaborate than the menu which is light and simple with usually a cold soup starter, a fish dish with vegetables from Highgrove and a sweet.

While the Prince hosts his own working dinners when scientists, architects and environmentalists gather to discuss matters which interest him, the royal couple occasionally entertain family and friends. Every autumn there is a dinner for his polo-playing partners while King Hussein and Crown Prince Hassan of Jordan are frequent guests when they are in town.

The rest of the royal family are not so fortunate. The Queen, Prince Philip, Princess Anne and Prince Edward rarely, if ever, come to call. While the Yorks and the Gloucesters are more frequent visitors, surprisingly it is Princess Margaret who spends the most time chatting over dinner with the Wales.

'Like Princess Margaret, Diana likes to mix with the stars after a show.'

Over the years Princess Margaret has rather taken Diana under her wing. She relinquished the patronages of Barnardo's and the English National Ballet in favour of the younger Princess while Diana has undertaken several engagements for her when she was ill. On Diana's arrival home from hospital with baby Prince William, it was Princess Margaret who organized the staff to welcome her back. They all furiously waved a motley assortment of tea towels and clothes as she pulled up outside apartments 8 and 9 carrying William in her arms.

Perhaps it is because the Princess sees a kindred spirit in Diana that she has taken such a keen interest in her royal progress. Like Diana, Princess Margaret is a metropolitan royal who loves the bright lights, the first nights and the chatter of the crush bar at the theatre and ballet. Her love of the arts was measured against the yardstick of a family who are resolutely and rustically middlebrow. This century has seen a monarchy wedded to the shires rather than the city. Those who prefer Sheridan to shooting, poetry to pheasants and ballet to Balmoral are

When the Princess entertains at Kensington Palace, dinner parties are formal, black-tie gatherings. Aristocrats, politicians, opera singers and film-makers have all enjoyed royal hospitality.

in a suspect minority at the Court of Queen Elizabeth II.

The tradition of philistinism in the Windsors, epitomized by the occasion when George VI threw a book at a courtier for daring to suggest that he should attend the opera more often, is still the dominant characteristic of the dynasty. At a recent Covent Garden gala Prince Philip and Prince Andrew took it in turns to retire to the back of the Royal Box so that they could enjoy an hour's sleep in between acts. Their frequent appearances and disappearances baffled newspaper publisher Robert Maxwell who was seated in the box next door.

Now Princess Margaret, forever cast as the royal rebel, has handed over the metropolitan torch to the Princess of Wales. Diana is more fortunate. In an age of mass travel the public can relate to a holiday in Majorca more than three months in the far north of Scotland. Her enjoyment of swimming, tennis, dancing and the theatre or simply watching television are far more accessible and understandable pursuits than fox hunting or polo.

It means that when Diana goes out in the evening she is signalling the eventual dawn of a new era for the monarchy. If the Princess of Wales has her way the next century will see a royal style where urban pursuits, not rustic recreations, are king.

CHAPTER FIVE
When Duty Calls

Humour breaks the social ice. A shared joke creates a bond, a bridge of understanding between strangers. When a princess meets a pauper, humour is the common language. While the Princess of Wales is no Bette Midler, she instinctively realizes the value of humour to calm nerves and slacken social tension. When she walks into a room of people on a royal engagement, the sense of anxious anticipation is almost palpable, the ranks of smiling faces masking the apprehension felt inside.

Vivienne Parry, of the charity Birthright, has often witnessed this phenomenon and the aftermath of a visit by the Princess to a hospital ward, a day centre or a reception. She observes, 'Before an event you encounter the same problems. Any number of people want to know how to address her and I know exactly what is going to happen. When you send them away they are full of nerves. At the end of the visit their comments are invariably on the lines of "She's so natural and normal."'

'The Princess's ability is talking about ordinary things like taking a trip to a supermarket. However, the quality she has most is compassion. She is genuinely moved and genuinely interested when meeting the ninety-fourth mother and baby as the first.'

While her qualities of warmth and compassion shine through, so does her ability not to take the situation or herself too seriously. She once startled John Bliss, senior administrator of the Royal Academy of Music. He recalls, 'Now and again she can really stun you. Her teasing sense of humour comes through. I once said to her at the end of an event, "You can come again in six months' time." She fixed me

with a mischievous twinkle in her eye and replied, "What if I'm pregnant Mr Bliss?" I was a little taken aback but I just answered, "Ma'am, we'll take you as we find you."'

It is the gulf between the image of a princess and the ordinary human being which many find disconcerting. On a visit to a Manchester hospital she joked about her slim shape when she was shown a £500,000 ($850,000) breast scanner. 'Gosh, you would have some difficulty getting much of me in there,' she remarked, much to the surprise of hospital staff.

At a lunch held in London's Carlton Tower hotel it was Diana who had to try and keep a straight face when a suave Frenchman addressed her as 'Your Royal 'ighness' and kept shooting her looks of smouldering Gallic charm. His flattery had the reverse effect of his intention. Diana said afterwards, 'It was so funny. He reminded me of the man in the Cointreau drinks commercial.' She insists she is not some porcelain princess to be placed on a pedestal. However, some royal organizers have yet to get the message. They will put her in a lift when she would prefer to walk and force royal photographers to march up endless flights of steps carrying heavy equipment. As one aide remarks, 'Diana could bound up the steps but the sight of these cameramen struggling up the stairs, unfit and out of breath, does make her smile. It is a small form of punishment for the things they do to her.'

Flags and flowers are a familiar part of a royal visit. Diana has the knack of sending everyone home feeling happy. Her relaxed manner and sense of humour soon put people at their ease.

Organization is at the heart of a royal visit, a prospect which generates thousands of man hours and many memos. Before the Princess arrives at a given venue every inch of the route has been timed and every room and corridor examined by police in boiler suits. Days of diplomatic work behind the scenes take place in order to strike the delicate balance between a visit paying lip service to the local worthies and allowing the Princess to see the work in progress. All too often royal visits are ruined by men in uniform and dignatories in chains.

Turning Point project manager, Nick Mounsey, gives a flavour of this painstaking process during the build-up to the Princess's visit to the Church Road Drug Project in Edgbaston. He wrote in the charity's magazine: 'When the date was confirmed, meetings gathered momentum with Turning Point's PR think tank coming firmly into focus. Provisional lists of who does what, where and at what time were established. Meetings took place, small, large and extremely large, each meeting begat more and more walkthroughs. We covered the royal route from perspectives of access, non-duplication, interest and security. The various organizational wrinkles were ironed out and the package given the suitability nod after a delightful visit by the lady-in-waiting.'

> ## 'A royal visit brings out the worst in people beforehand and the best while it is taking place.'

It means that before the statutory bouquet is handed to Diana, there will have been wrangling, sometimes acrimonious, over who will finally meet her, what she will see and how she will see it. A royal visit brings out the worst in people beforehand but the best while it is taking place.

However, as Diana sips a cup of Earl Grey tea over breakfast at Kensington Palace, this bickering, backbiting and social climbing is reduced to a couple of sheets of A4 notepaper. It contains a working schedule, a summary of the visit, as well as names and brief biographies of the people she

is due to meet in the course of a working day which can start at 8 o'clock in the morning and go on until nearly midnight.

The Princess is able to read between the lines of these briefings which can often be too reverential. Before she visited the Manchester branch of Birthright her briefing stated that the secretary, Norma Atkinson, was suffering from cancer. During the reception she found organizer Vivienne Parry and said to her, 'I know I haven't met her yet. Which one is she?' Diana made a point of singling her out and spending some time with her. She realized instinctively that Mrs Atkinson, who died within days of the visit, had literally clung on to life in order to meet the Princess.

No polite resumé can ever express the hidden stories behind so many of her visits. The knowledge that so much time and effort goes into arranging a visit means that the Princess, and the rest of the royal family, have almost a duty to stay healthy. As one member of staff recalls, 'The Princess has never forgotten the upset and disappointment people felt when she cancelled an engagement during her pregnancy with Prince Harry. The result is that if a member of staff has a cold or something they are told to keep clear.'

This conscientious professionalism was demonstrated to Vivienne Parry when the Princess visited a leisure centre in Holywell, North Wales. Vivienne recalls, 'She was laughing hysterically as she watched the children trying to look fierce as they practised their karate. It was the day before Major Hugh Lindsay's funeral and anyone could have forgiven her for being down. But the show must go on.'

Before she boards her helicopter or gets into her chauffeur-driven Jaguar, the Princess is aware that while she may face a routine day's engagements, it will be an experience treasured for a lifetime by those about to meet her.

Just before she departs the Princess has a brief meeting with her private secretary, Patrick Jephson, to discuss any last-minute changes. Hiccups do occur, however. When she made a private visit to the Passage Day Centre for the Homeless last year, police sniffer dogs went through the building looking for explosives and weapons. A couple of teenage inmates, worried

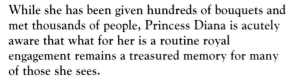

While she has been given hundreds of bouquets and met thousands of people, Princess Diana is acutely aware that what for her is a routine royal engagement remains a treasured memory for many of those she sees.

that their Bowie knives would be confiscated, handed them to Sister Barbara, who runs the centre. Sister Barbara recalls, 'I was with the Princess during the entire visit walking round carrying these concealed weapons. No one was ever the wiser.'

At a Kensington Palace reception for Turning Point, the charity concerned with drug and alcohol abuse, she was briefed on the Griffith Report and its implications for the National Health Service and care in the community. Other meetings at Kensington Palace have dealt with everything from cerebral palsy in children to the internal struggles facing the English National Ballet.

Besides informal lunches and meetings with charity officials, the Princess is also using her London home as a centre to launch appeals. It can be a tricky business. When Barnardo's asked her if she would sign a 'Children's Charter' she arranged for three mentally handicapped youngsters to sit with her during the ceremony. Curiosity got the better of Gerald, a teenager from Northern Ireland, who insisted on looking round the rest of the apartment. The Princess

showed him the butler's pantry and nearby rooms while Roger Singleton marshalled the other youngsters in preparation for a polite departure. He recalls, 'Just at the point when I was looking across to Anne Beckwith-Smith for that "time to go" signal Gerald grabbed my hand and said to the Princess, "I've got to go now." And that was that. The reason was that he had been promised the front place in the bus and didn't want to miss it.'

Gerald, seated left, enjoyed his visit to Kensington Palace so much that, after the Princess had launched the Children's Charter on behalf of Barnardo's, he insisted on a guided tour.

Diana is shouldering a greater burden of royal duties, performing on average an engagement at least every working day of the year. As her boys grow up and move away to school, she will take on even more responsibilities. Why does she do it? She does not receive an allowance from the Civil List, the public monies paid to the royal family to pay for the staff and administration costs of running the monarchy, and the demands of a growing family could excuse all but the bare minimum of public duties. Indeed she is independent from all obligation, having her own family trust fund, supplemented by a substantial bequest left by her American great-grandmother Frances Work, as well as an allowance from the Duchy of Cornwall estates.

However, she does feel the wider obligation, a sense of service to the community and the nation. *Noblesse oblige* has been the accepted tradition within the Spencer family, whose motto is 'God Defend the Right', while the Prince of Wales's motto, 'I serve', neatly encapsulates the royal family's sense of duty to the country.

While the Princess accepts these conventions as the framework for her role in society her profound dedication to the values of family life goes beyond accepted orthodoxies. Her own childhood, dominated by memories of a tran-

The Princess combines professional interest with the personal touch, as she gently adjusts the bow-tie of one lucky youngster.

sient series of nannies and scarred by a bitter divorce, may be a partial explanation for her thoughtful interest in the family. Indeed while her own marriage may not have brought lasting happiness it has at least given her the security she cherishes.

As one friend says, 'While the newness of performing the job has gone, she does have a commitment to certain values of family life. It may be considered old-fashioned but she firmly believes in the family as the basis for stability in life and society at large.'

For example her work for Relate, the marriage-guidance counselling service, started as curiosity and has rapidly mushroomed so that she now takes an active part in counselling sessions and, on at least one occasion, has attended a private session at the charity's Rugby headquarters where Relate trainee counsellors role-play various domestic conflicts.

Relate's director, David French, remarks, 'The trainees did not know when they signed up for the course that the Princess would be attending. It is a great tribute to her personal skills that it was anything but disruptive. She is a very perceptive and intuitive person. It is a great gift especially in the role she is destined to play. Even the sceptics among our counsellors acknowledge that she would make a very good addition to our team because she is such a natural communicator.'

Her concern for family life is one of the threads of her public work, caring for the victims in society is another. Her work with Aids patients, lepers, drug addicts and sexually abused children has brought her in contact with undesirable problems in the community, and issues which have no easy solutions.

When Sister Barbara walked round the centre for the homeless she administers, she was able to observe the Princess and her instinctive empathy. She recalls, 'She is seriously concerned about homelessness. There is a great dignity in the way she meets people and sits down and talks to them. The Princess mixes very easily with people. We have former clerics, accountants, artists and writers here, people for whom life has gone wrong and cannot get their lives back together. The Princess was very caring in a way that was very refreshing.'

With characteristic understatement, Jimmy Savile calls her a 'miracle worker' and pinpoints the visit she made to the hysterectomy ward at Stoke Mandeville hospital. He recalls, 'It is not normally included on visits for VIPs. When we arrived at the ward she was confronted by thirty beds. Not only did she talk to every patient but she sat on every bed to do so. I think that shows her true nature. It epitomized Diana. It wasn't a glamour ward and it wasn't a cosmetic appearance but she did it because it is in her. She is magic, a very real person.'

Her aristocratic background and her caring nature are not the only forces which motivate her actions. She is acutely aware that she has influence. A picture of Diana shaking hands with an Aids patient is worth a hundred articles, a royal word has great resonance and a royal presence generates millions of pounds in donations to her charities.

As one Aids patient told her when she toured a ward in London's St Mary's Hospital, 'A handshake from you is worth 100,000 words from us. You are a leader and you have helped society to wake up to the issues.' In a similar way she has tried to use her global appeal to peel away the myths surrounding leprosy when she shook the hands of sufferers in Nigeria and Indonesia. Her tours of hospital wards and clinics help to highlight the problems of addiction, be it smoking, drink or drugs, while her visits to the headquarters of Childline, a free telephone link for children in danger of abuse, has brought this twilight issue into the open.

While the handsome cheques from the charity balls and premières she attends are encouraging, the human fall-out from her work provides the most satisfaction. Toddler Annabel Fox, now two years old, has a special reason to thank the Princess. Her mother Liz Fox, who had suffered several miscarriages, was inspired to make one final attempt to start a family when she saw the Princess on television visiting a new hospital unit which pioneered treatment for women like her. Liz Fox, who lives in Poole in Dorset, says, 'Annabel really is our miracle and it is all thanks to Diana and the care of some wonderful doctors and nurses.'

Indeed words like 'miracle', 'natural gift' and 'a real-life saint' regularly fall from the lips of

Reach out and touch. A royal handshake is sometimes more than a simple greeting. It can help dispel the myths surrounding diseases like Aids and leprosy.

those who meet the Princess, endowing her with almost quasi-religious powers. Doctors, not known for their sentimentality in the face of suffering, are impressed by her approach. Consultant Peter Gautier-Smith of the National Hospital's rehabilitation homes, says, 'She seems to have extraordinary healing powers. You could almost compare it with the laying on of hands. The uplift which the Princess gives the patient she visits can sometimes do more good than any doctor.'

Perhaps the most vivid example of Diana's impact occurred in the aftermath of the Manchester air disaster where a teenage girl opened her eyes for the first time when the Princess toured her hospital. The Princess's work inspired artist André Durand to paint her as an 'angel of mercy' bringing relief to sufferers in an Aids ward.

As platitudes and princesses are inevitable bedfellows, it is often difficult to tease out the truth from the illusion and self-delusion. She is not a saint, as the American magazine *Vanity Fair* described her, nor is she a saviour. As the Princess says, 'I am deeply embarrassed when people put me on a pedestal. It is just ridiculous.'

The use of such hyperbole devalues both the words themselves and belittles the work of doctors, nurses and others who are involved in the daily emotional grind of dealing with Aids patients, drug addicts and other victims of disease and society. Diana does, of course, have her off days when she is uncooperative with cameramen and when she appears bored and distracted. In fairness her moodiness usually occurs after a bout of negative media publicity and her boredom when she has to tour soulless factories. She is essentially a people's Princess.

However it is undeniable that the Princess has an effect over and above the usual excitement generated by a VIP visit. 'The biggest single benefit from having the Princess of Wales as our President is the pleasure that individual visits give to the people involved,' says Roger Singleton of Barnardo's. 'The parents of physically handicapped children, who may be dribbling or be a bit of a mess, have a finely tuned instinct for the reaction of other adults. They watch the Princess particularly closely. She passes that critical test. The Princess accepts these youngsters no matter how bent or buckled they may be.'

It is an instant morale boost. After a visit to Sheffield in Yorkshire the parent of one handicapped child said proudly, 'If my kid is good enough for the Princess of Wales, then she is good enough for anybody.'

She has the ability to create a cocoon of intimacy around her in spite of the hovering photographers, bodyguards and Lord Lieutenants. Roger Singleton was particularly impressed by her technique during a visit to Salford, Greater Manchester. He recalls, 'She got down on her knees and talked to the parents of a handicapped youngster who was prone to fits. She asked if they had any other children and

when they said that they didn't feel that they could she then asked them how the presence of a handicapped child had affected their marriage. Somehow she creates the atmosphere where people can talk about their most personal and intimate details.'

Her personable, down-to-earth approach was observed by Valerie Howarth, executive director of Childline, when the Princess met two abused youngsters during a visit to the charity's headquarters. She says, 'She is so remarkably relaxed and has that extraordinary ability to relate to people. She doesn't make you feel that she is more important than the rest of the world.' Indeed her involvement with Childline admirably illustrates the happy collision of fortune, interest and action which characterizes Diana's charitable work. Her interest in child abuse was sparked by the Cleveland scandal which involved scores of parents and their children in the north-east of England. She felt so strongly about the subject that, after discussion with Roger Singleton at a charity dinner, she raised the matter at a Barnardo's council meeting.

Brave Dawn Rogers presents a book containing pictures of handicapped British children being treated at the famed Peto Institute in Budapest, Hungary. British doctors thought that Dawn, aged nine, would spend the rest of her life in a wheelchair; now she can walk unaided.

By chance the television personality and Childline chairman, Esther Rantzen, highlighted the problem in a documentary which the Princess happened to be watching. She sent a 'substantial' personal donation followed up by two trips to the charity's London headquarters.

During her visits she has sat next to counsellors who man the telephones twenty-four hours a day and talk to children who call for help. It can be a harrowing experience.. During her first visit she stood by a counsellor as she tried to talk to a young girl who was being abused by her stepfather. As she poured out her troubles, the youngster was forced to cut short her call when she heard her stepfather moving about in the bedroom upstairs. It was a chilling moment which graphically underlined the need for the service. 'Princess Diana was very moved,' said Esther Rantzen. 'You could see it in her eyes. She listened with enormous intensity.'

At the same time Diana's involvement has raised the charity's profile, increased donations and enabled Childline to install additional telephone lines and open extra centres so that more youngsters can call for advice. Professional compassion combined with practical action is the public face of the Princess of Wales.

This public image is matched by the private reality. During a stay at Balmoral she made a special visit to see Linda Murdoch, the widow of royal baker, Ken Murdoch, who was tragically killed in an horrific car accident. After the Klosters tragedy she befriended Sarah Lindsay, the widow of Major Hugh Lindsay who was killed in the avalanche. Since then the two mothers have forged a close bond – Sarah and her daughter, Alice, were invited to Prince Harry's birthday party at Kensington Palace while Sarah regularly accompanies the Princess on evening outings to the theatre and concerts.

Immediately she heard of the death of Lily Snipp, her former school piano and dance teacher, she sent a letter of condolence to her niece. Her letter, on Sandringham notepaper, said simply: 'I wanted to say how *very* sorry I was to hear about your aunt, Miss Snipp. It must have come as a dreadful shock to you and your family – the very least I can do is to send you my deepest sympathy and to say that I am thinking of you and your family at this unhappy time . . .

Tree planting and royalty go hand in hand. The Princess undertakes a routine task with enthusiasm and humour.

Words are such inadequate things to express what one really wants to say, but I did so want you to know how sad I was and to add that I greatly appreciated you taking the trouble to write to me when I know that you must have a lot on your mind at the moment. Thank you for thinking of me.'

As one of Diana's friends says, 'She really is one of the most caring people I know.' That streak of sympathy enables the Princess to surmount the usual obstacles of protocol when she feels the impulse to reach out and help. She sent a comforting note to Dawn Griffiths, a mother whose baby was stolen from St Thomas' Hospital in London by a bogus social worker, and made a surprise Christmas visit to St Bride's Church in Fleet Street to join the family of the television cameraman John McCarthy currently held hostage in Beirut.

95

During a surprise visit to Northern Ireland the Princess shared a joke with soldiers from the Royal Hampshire Regiment, of which she is Colonel-in-Chief.

She told the kidnap victim's father, 'I want you to know how much I feel for you at this time. I pray for you and your family all the time.' Again when she heard the news about the sinking of the *Marchioness* cruiser on the River Thames she immediately offered to attend the memorial service for the young people drowned and help comfort the bereaved. 'She gave us hope and strength to carry on,' said one grieving mother afterwards.

While her genuinely sympathetic nature is revealed in her spontaneous response to tragedy, her professional interest in social problems emerges in a pattern of private visits she now undertakes. These secret excursions enable her to become involved in the issues without the attendant officials and media creating a barrier to understanding.

Les Rudd, chief executive of Turning Point, organized a private visit to the Roma centre in Hammersmith, west London so that she could meet seriously unstable young people in conditions approaching normality. When she arrived seventeen young people, several dressed in colourful punk gear, were in the middle of a discussion group. Les Rudd recalls, 'They weren't at all worried by her presence. It was a very lively discussion and they were challenging her all the time, asking her questions. They wanted to know how it felt to be a mother and a woman continually under the spotlight. In a curious way they could relate to her because when they are outside in society they too are treated as a sideshow.' Such was the spirited rapport that at the end of her visit they dragged her into a football-style team photo.

A rather more formal welcome faced her when she arrived at the Tottenham, north London home of Bangie and Beryl Pringle for tea and rum cake. She wanted to learn more about how the couple have successfully fostered three youngsters all of whom were considered 'unfosterable'. However, it was the Princess who was faced with a barrage of questions as she chatted about her schooldays, her cooking abilities – 'Hopeless at sauces' – and how she failed her driving test the first time round.

Aside from the banter, she was able to seriously discuss the issues of adoption and fostering with the Pringles in a relaxed, informal way that could never have been achieved on a royal visit. After the visit Beryl observed, 'She is a friendly person, somebody I could sit down with and have a proper discussion and get somewhere. She is not a stuck-up type.' Since then she has made three entirely private visits – on one occasion she waited patiently in the sitting room of a London foster home for the adopted daughter to arrive home from school in order to understand the human problems behind the policy issues.

Indeed the deeper she becomes involved in her charities, the more she has become interested in the wider implications of the social issues facing her. Her speeches on family life, on drug and alcohol abuse and the problems of old age are ways in which she is articulating her general concerns. Even with the help of film producer Sir Richard Attenborough, her style is hesitant but heartfelt. Like most people she has a horror of public speaking and at the end of her speech she often turns to her staff or a member of the press she knows and mouths, 'Was that alright?' her cheeks flushed with nervous adrenalin.

Les Rudd of Turning Point observes, 'She is not going to speak very often and she is nervous in the way that anyone would be but she is now beginning to enjoy it. She is aware of her position, aware that she has been portrayed as a clothes horse and she is making a statement for herself.'

The Princess, who failed her driving test at the first attempt, moved on to bigger things when she took the wheel of a double-decker bus on a trip to Hong Kong.

'She is heir to the heritage of dignified but personable royal service exemplified by the Queen Mother.'

She can gain comfort in the knowledge that, in their twenties and early thirties, Prince Charles and Princess Anne were awkward speechmakers, both in delivery and content. The precedents are clear. As both these royals have grown in maturity and expertise, they have felt able to speak out on controversial issues. Architecture, income tax, the environment and overseas aid are some of the issues they have addressed.

The signs are that Princess Diana will follow suit. 'You can only do so many visits before you start asking serious questions about how these issues relate to the wider community,' notes Les Rudd. She now has a number of patronages which give her an overview of family life in Britain which few government ministers or charity executives could boast.

Her work with Relate, Turning Point, Help the Aged, Childline and Barnardo's place her in a unique position of influence to see the relationships between child abuse, marital breakdown, homelessness and drug addiction in the wider context of family life. Inevitably she will be drawn into controversy. As Roger Singleton says, 'As she gains more experience in these interlocking areas she will speak out more and these views may not accord with current government policy.'

That is for the future. At present she is heir to the heritage of dignified but personable royal service exemplified by the Queen Mother. As John Bliss says, 'The Princess is an absolute poppet. She has great charm and like the Queen Mother she has the same knack of making you feel important and that she is interested in you. The Princess is the natural successor to the Queen Mother in the people's affections. She is a great asset to the country.'

There can be no finer tribute to a Princess who finds her public duty as fulfilling for herself as it is a pleasure for the many who meet her.

CHAPTER SIX
Calendar Girl

She did not look much like a future queen and neither did she feel like becoming one. As Lady Diana Spencer stood in the middle of a muddy field at Nobottle Wood on the Althorp estate the last thing on her mind was romance. On that bleak November day she would have swapped the world for a warm drink and a hot bath as she waited disconsolately for the next drive of pheasants.

Her appearance was as woebegone as her spirits. She was wearing an ill-fitting anorak borrowed from her sister Sarah, a Marks and Spencer checked shirt, a pair of cords and the ubiquitous green Hunter wellington boots. As the afternoon wore on endlessly the plump-cheeked teenager began to regret having asked her headmistress for a special weekend away from school simply because the Prince of Wales was making his first visit to the family home.

If she was out to impress the Prince she could not have cut a more disconsolate figure, her hair as untidy as her marksmanship. 'She was a pathetic shot, simply dreadful,' recalls one of the shooting party, adding with emphasis, 'And she was only using a single bore gun.' If, as Sarah McCorquodale has since confessed, the reason behind Prince Charles's invitation was to allow a little matchmaking between himself and her kid sister, then the omens were hardly auspicious.

When Prince Charles returned to his room in the majestic stately home he found that he could not open the windows – he loves fresh air – and then that he could not find his bath, which

Alone with her thoughts, the most photographed woman in the world is in a reflective mood as she looks out across the Caribbean.

he enjoys even more. After an hour wandering around the corridors in his dressing gown, the Prince was in a foul mood when he finally located the butler. So he was not best pleased when the butler pointed out that his bath was incorporated in the fitted wardrobes inside his bedroom. Charles, who likes to luxuriate in the tub, had to make do with a quick dip before joining Queen Margherita of Denmark, known in the family as 'Daisy Dane', and the Spencer sisters for dinner.

However, a romantic spark must have been ignited as Charles's first memories of Diana on that fateful weekend are of 'a very jolly and amusing and attractive sixteen-year-old – full of fun'.

While not all weekend shooting parties have such historic consequences a customary feature is that the best 'bags' are often made at the dinner table rather than on the 'killing fields'. The house party is a prominent feature of the aristocracy's social calendar, a yearly rhythm of engagements that has altered little since Queen Victoria's day. Indeed if Queen Victoria were alive now she would note with satisfaction that the Court still continues its annual round of Christmas at Sandringham, Easter at Windsor Castle, Ascot in June and the summer holiday on the royal estates at Balmoral. 'You could almost set your watch by their behaviour,' notes one former employee.

Shooting weekends are still as much a part of Diana's social diary for the winter months as is Ascot during the summer. When the Wales go away for the weekend they are entertained by nobility and attended by servants in the finest suite the stately home or castle has to offer.

At least that is the theory. On one occasion Prince Charles arrived very late at Blenheim Palace, the home of the Duke of Marlborough. He was exhausted after spending the evening at an RAF dinner and was desperate to get to bed. However his party arrived to find the house in darkness. The Duke, weary of waiting for the Prince of Wales, had retired. After hammering on the front door for several minutes, the door was reluctantly opened by the deaf Spanish housekeeper who spoke little English. Eventually the Prince, in an ill humour, found his way to his bedroom. He left early the following day, unimpressed by the Duke's hospitality.

Normally the arrangements for a royal visit are more predictable than the weather. If their hosts are close friends – like the Duke of Roxburghe, the Duke and Duchess of Westminster and Lord and Lady Romsey – they will know the personal preferences of the royal couple. Where there is any doubt a host will send the menu and other details to St James's Palace for approval. Hours before the royal couple are expected, Diana's dresser and Charles's valet will travel ahead in a royal estate car, sometimes with a police car. They unpack their luggage, lay out their evening clothes and organize their rooms the way they like them.

Prince Charles, here watched by the Queen Mother, is one of the finest shots in Britain and treasures his pair of Purdey guns which were bequeathed to him by George VI. At times he is so quick that his loaders cannot keep up.

It was during a shooting weekend on the Spencer estate that Charles and Diana began their romance. However, Diana is not keen on the sport, often joining the men for lunch and then driving back to the main house.

When the Prince and Princess arrive, their hosts and staff are waiting on the steps to greet them. Then, with a flurry of curtsies and bows, the party moves inside. Formality reigns supreme when royalty comes to call. Dinner parties are black-tie affairs, perhaps with a local bishop or Lord Lieutenant as a guest. However, if they are really close friends, like the Romseys, then the dinner party is more relaxed and games are often on the menu for after-dinner jollity. These late-night diversions hail from an age when television was not invented and people made their own entertainment. Charades and bobbing for apples in a bucket are favoured after-dinner pursuits. Diana and Charles are happy to play hide-and-seek and the curious sport of biting the rabbit's tail. This is where a lady pins a tail to a chosen part of her anatomy and then runs around the room chased by the men who try and pull it off with their teeth. 'When you have seen the Prince of Wales playing this you have to pinch yourself to make sure you are still in the twentieth century,' notes one observer drily. No matter how ribald the company becomes, decorum decrees that the host and hostess may not retire until the Prince and Princess decide to go to bed.

Another golden rule is that the royal family never eats breakfast with other people. It is tradition and customs are there to be kept. So Diana and Charles eat in their bedroom suite, Charles in semi-shooting gear of plus fours, open-necked shirt and slippers and Diana in a simple day dress. The Prince likes poached eggs and milk before a shoot, Diana makes do with toast and Earl Grey tea.

Prince Charles is undoubtedly one of the finest shots in Britain, his marksmanship and speed renowned in shooting circles. It is a skill he has inherited from his great-grandfather, George V, who could blaze away all day on the Sandringham estate and never miss a bird. Charles inherited a pair of perfect Purdey shotguns from his grandfather George VI, the polished stock emblazoned with the late King's initials and the Prince of Wales feathers. Indeed stories that said he had given his Purdeys to the Duke of York were as ludicrous as the tales which suggested he had given up shooting. The Prince has such a keen eye and fast reflexes that sometimes his loaders cannot keep up.

Depending on the weather, Diana, who has several woollen Edwardian-style outfits she wears on the butts, will stand by the side of the Prince watching the slaughter. But sometimes the Princess and the other ladies will arrive just before lunch. After lunch the ladies stay on with their menfolk and accompany the shoot before heading back to the main house for a bath, drinks in the drawing room and discussion over dinner of the day's events.

On Sunday the Queen, the Queen Mother and the older members of the royal family go to church. When the Wales are staying with friends they do not bother unless there is a private chapel in the grounds. The Prince and Princess argue, with good reason, that going to church is the equivalent of a royal engagement with all the attendant security. It turns a day of rest into a working day, not just for themselves, but also for the local constabulary. The guns are silent, members of the house party going for an hour's riding or taking the children for a walk in the grounds.

While Sunday lunch is not as formal as dinner, the company still wear suits or their best tweeds before sitting down to a three-course meal. The afternoon is a truly private time with nothing formally organized for the royal guests.

When the royal couple take their leave late on Sunday afternoon they know that they will soon be seeing their friends again. The Prince and Princess host at least one shooting weekend

before Christmas on the Sandringham estate, still one of the finest pheasant shoots in the country. While the 'bags' – the number of birds and wildlife shot – are not as high as in the days of Edward VII when 3,000 pheasants a day was common, the tally is still a respectable 500 or so birds.

Guests arrive on the Thursday for a weekend's shooting and the form is very similar to a shoot on their own estates. But there are a few distinctions which add a certain style to a stay at the Queen's 20,000-acre estate. Liveried footmen are on hand to attend to the gentlemen while Diana's hairdresser, Richard Dalton, is available for the lady guests.

A shooting lunch on the Queen's Norfolk estate is also an unusual occasion, usually situated in the Sandringham or Anmer church hall. These are bleak, chilly barns, their only decoration being cheap yellowing pictures of King George V and the Queen Mary. In this incongruous setting various crowned and exiled European monarchs and princes will lunch, served by frozen footmen dressed in scarlet livery.

Their meal is brought in a trailer specially designed by Prince Philip. Inside there are compartments for silver, plate and hot and cold food. The royals, who eat off plastic plates seated at wooden trestle tables, are served home-

Every year the royal couple host a shooting weekend at Sandringham; a visit to church on Sunday morning is part of the ritual.

made vegetable soup, salads, cold meats, jacket potatoes in silver foil and cheese from the Windsor dairy. While coffee and tea are on offer, most of the company, including the royals, like a glass of sloe gin to warm them through after a morning standing in ploughed fields. In the afternoon, the Princess often brings Princes William and Harry to watch the action and help collect the birds.

For a woman who does not list hunting and shooting high on her list of priorities, time at Sandringham can hang heavily. However, Diana and the Duchess of York have recently discovered a health and fitness centre near the estate where they go for regular swimming sessions and workouts in the gym.

Curiously Sandringham does not have a swimming pool or tennis courts. This has now been rectified at Balmoral. For years the Princess and her children had to ask a local hotel for permission to use their pool. While the management were happy to oblige, the procedure involved undignified scuffles with waiting photographers and complaints from hotel guests. Now the Queen has decided to build a pool on the estate to cater for the activities of the younger royal generation whose hearts do not soar at the prospect of long days on the grouse moors, chilly picnics by the banks of Loch Muick or crawling through the heather in search of stags.

Charles revels in his days amid the purple heather and the brooding hills. Diana who prefers the city lights to Balmoral knows the timetable of the British Airways Aberdeen to London shuttle off by heart. Diana is in good company for neither Lord Snowdon, Princess Margaret's ex-husband, nor Captain Mark Phillips, Princess Anne's estranged partner, shared the Windsors' love of their 40,000-acre estate. Even Edward VII called it a 'Highland barn with a thousand draughts'.

The first stage of the Queen's traditional summer break brings back the happiest memories for Princess Diana. This is when Prince Philip hosts a party on board the royal yacht *Britannia* in the Solent during the Cowes regatta. It was at one of these parties with guests that included Lady Sarah Armstrong-Jones and Susan Deptford, now married to the Duchess of

York's father, that Lady Diana Spencer and Prince Charles began their romance in earnest.

A Mediterranean honeymoon and cruises off the Canadian and Italian coasts have sealed Diana's affection for the 5,700-ton yacht. She is popular with the 276-strong yacht's company and has joined in sing-songs around the piano in the mess and visited the kitchens to chat to chef 'Swampie' Marsh and his colleagues. 'The Princess is very approachable,' says one rating who admires the fact that she remembers to send congratulations cards when ratings' wives have given birth.

It was on one such cruise that she drew a charming pencil sketch of Prince William on the back of a piece of *Britannia* headed notepaper. However, her drawing, now kept at Windsor Castle, was very nearly thrown away by an over-zealous steward who saw the piece of paper and, thinking it was scrap, threw it into the bin. Fortunately the Princess retrieved it for posterity.

'The yearly rhythm of engagements has altered little since Queen Victoria's day.'

The annual ten-day cruise around the Western Isles of Scotland officially starts when the Queen joins her yacht at Southampton and gives members of the royal family every opportunity to revive artistic talents. If the weather is good Prince Charles and Prince Philip like to go on deck for an afternoon's sketching. William and Harry, carefully monitored by ratings, have the run of the ship, playing on make-shift swings or joining in a game of deck hockey. During her childhood Princess Anne enjoyed her days on board so much that she brought her teddy bears, dolls and dolls' house because she thought the sea air would do them good.

While dinners are formal affairs – the royal family are serenaded by a 26-piece Royal Marine band as they enjoy a typical supper of salmon, lamb and chocolate profiteroles – lunch is invariably a picnic on a remote island off the Scottish coast. In the morning the Queen, in discussion with the yacht's captain, Rear Admiral John Garniere, will decide on a suitable site – last year a World War II bomb shelter in Lossiemouth was the distinctly unglamorous setting for one family picnic.

Before they disembark a small detachment from the Special Boat Squadron, the seaborne equivalent of the SAS, goes ashore, followed by several Scotland Yard detectives. The royal family value their privacy. During the cruise certain rituals are observed. The men are not permitted to wear a kilt until the yacht is north of Perth and the only time everyone is allowed on deck is when the royal yacht passes Duart Castle, the home of the late Lord MacLean. His staff would wave towels and sheets from the battlements as the royal yacht, sending flares into the afternoon sky, sailed past.

The other time-honoured ritual is the arrival of the yacht at Scrabster Harbour near the Queen Mother's Scottish home, the Castle of Mey. This is the only occasion in the year when the public can see the Windsors behave as both a family and a Court. At 11 o'clock sharp Diana and other members of the royal family disembark to greet the Queen Mother who waits at the top of the granite harbour steps. The traditional greeting of a full court curtsy and formal kissing on the cheeks and hand takes place watched by a thousand or so townsfolk and photographers. After the royal family has taken tea with the Queen Mother the yacht heads south, sending up maroons and flares as she makes her stately progress to Aberdeen where the Princess and the rest of the royal family disembark for the drive to Balmoral.

The Queen's holiday in Scotland lasts almost three months with a stream of guests invited to sample the delights of fishing on the Dee, shooting on the grouse moors above the village of Tomintoul and stag hunting in the shadow of Lochnagar.

Diana has tried to join in. She is said to have been 'blooded' by a ghillie when she shot her first stag. This is an age-old ritual where the animal's heart is cut out and its blood smeared over the successful marksman's face. But she can hardly be described as an enthusiast. Indeed these days she is more often seen with a camera in her hand than a shotgun. She prefers to take

Diana plays by the banks of the River Dee with Prince Harry. However, Balmoral holds few attractions for the Princess, who spends as little time as possible at the Queen's Highland retreat.

her children for walks along the banks of the River Dee, watch William racing around in his electric go-kart, or drive to the nearby town of Ballater to do some shopping. While she may suffer the dubious joys of the Highland retreat through gritted teeth – she always gives friends a wry smile when they ask about her Scottish holidays – the events on the Balmoral social calendar she always enjoys are the Ghillies' Balls held in the Castle's great hall. One year she joined in the boisterous Highland reels with such abandon that she ripped the hem of her evening gown when a fellow dancer stepped on it. On these occasions the royal family dance with their staff, estate workers and the ghillies.

The Princess had to tread very diplomatically when she suggested to Prince Charles that they

Above: While the Queen and Queen Mother take a keen interest in the children's sack race at the Braemar Games, the Princess chats to her husband.

Right: The Princess is a familiar face in Ballater, the nearest village to Balmoral. The High Street is adorned with numerous 'By Appointment' signs.

accept an invitation from King Juan Carlos to join him on the holiday island of Majorca as opposed to spending the entire summer at the traditional Balmoral retreat. While Marivent Palace, where the royal couple and their children stayed, is within range of photographers as is the private military beach where Diana took the children paddling it has not prevented them from making several visits. The Prince, as ever, does his own thing, driving into the hills for a day's sketching. 'I did some of my best work there,' he recalled during a cocktail reception in Madrid. However, it was noticeable that he returned to bracing Balmoral several days earlier than the Princess who headed back to London.

In the early years of their married life they went on several holidays together. They enjoyed a winter break at King Hussein of Jordan's beach-front palace in Aqaba, skiied every year with friends and even visited Eleuthera, the Caribbean island which became notorious for sneak photographs of the pregnant Princess.

Apart from a short break at Charles's holiday home on Tamarisk in the Isles of Scilly where they took the boys cycling around the narrow lanes, the royal couple have not enjoyed many family holidays. The Prince's love affair with Italy – he even employed an Italian chef for a year to teach Mervyn Wycherley how to make pasta – has grown to such a degree that he has been given the use of a splendid villa in Tuscany for an architects' summer school. He invariably goes on his own, leaving Diana to do her own thing in London.

Since the Klosters tragedy when the Queen's former equerry, Major Hugh Lindsay, was killed in an avalanche, the Princess has decided against joining her husband on the slopes. Neither did she accompany him on the private visits he made to Turkey and southern Africa. On one occasion he was camping in the Kalahari Desert with his friend, Sir Laurens van der Post, when a pair of lions made a late foray around his tent, leaving with two plastic buckets.

These days it is a classier version of the traditional bucket-and-spade holiday which attracts the Princess. For the last two years she has been a guest of millionaire Richard Branson at his private island of Necker, 60 miles east of Puerto Rico in the Caribbean. Branson, who

> ## 'The chance to join the rich in their playgrounds and play with their toys is one which Diana enjoys.'

owns a multi-million-dollar music and airline business, was happy to waive the usual £5,300 ($9,000) a day charge and even had his island declared a Crown possession for the visits.

It is a true paradise where jet-set pop stars like Paul McCartney, Phil Collins and actor Robert De Niro have enjoyed the privacy and hospitality afforded by the extrovert tycoon. Before Branson lavished thousands of pounds on making the 74-acre island habitable, Necker had been abandoned because the snake-infested wasteland was not fit to live on. On her first visit, with her two sisters, their seven children and her mother, the Princess took full advantage of the opportunity to relax in the winter sun.

The chance to join the rich in their playgrounds is one which the Princess clearly enjoys.

This ambition is no different from that of, say, Princess Caroline of Monaco or Queen Noor of Jordan who move in the rarefied atmosphere inhabited by the global jet set. It does however sit uncomfortably with a family who spend so much of their leisure hours in time-honoured aristocratic pursuits. The week the Princess spent at Champneys health farm reveals her metropolitan rather than her rustic instincts. It is hard to imagine Princess Anne giving up her riding and shooting activities for a week of pampered luxury.

There is, however, no escaping the annual Christmas and New Year pilgrimage to Sandringham. Her father, Earl Spencer, may grumble that he would like to see his grandchildren on Christmas Day but when the Court moves to the Norfolk estate the Princess of Wales must follow her Sovereign. Diana is, above all, a dutiful Princess.

Indeed, Christmas sees Diana wearing four different 'hats' as an employer, wife of the local squire, a mother and a princess. As employers she and Prince Charles start Christmas early. If

Princess Diana is always happy to join King Juan Carlos and his family at his palace on Majorca. The royal party go for regular cruises on board his yacht, *Fortuna (left)*. Although she enjoys skiing *(below left)*, Diana has still to regain her nerve for the sport following the Klosters tragedy when a member of Prince Charles's party was killed in an avalanche. She is on safer ground as she directs Prince William along the lanes around Tamarisk in the Isles of Scilly *(below)*.

they have a long flight for their autumn foreign tour they will use the time profitably to sign a host of the thousand or so Christmas cards they send out annually. When it is a joint card the Prince puts the recipient's name at the top, writes 'Best wishes' or 'Thanks for all your help' and then signs it. Diana simply writes her name in her familiar flowing hand.

With all Good Wishes
for Christmas
and the New Year

Charles and Diana.

On long flights the royal couple fill the hours by writing their Christmas cards.

They also play host to luncheon or drinks parties for members of the Royal Protection Squad and the staffs of Kensington Palace and the Highgrove estate. One year it was held at Coutts, the royal bankers, on another occasion all the staff had lunch at Kensington Palace. Now their Household is so large that they have separate parties for their different homes.

Spontaneity is not a hallmark of these get-togethers. Several weeks beforehand the Wales' staff are given a £20 ($34) bonus and told to buy and wrap their own present. In return they have £3 ($5.1) taken from their wages to buy a gift for the Prince and Princess which is presented at a teatime drinks party. Then the royal couple go through the absurd ritual of handing back the presents which the staff have bought and wrapped themselves. However the staff do receive the added bonus of a Christmas pudding.

The nearby town of Tetbury is not neglected in the build-up to Christmas. Charles and Diana play host to local pensioners who are shown around the garden and the local choir is invited to sing carols around the Christmas tree in the hall. When the last verse of 'O, Come All Ye Faithful' fades away, William and Harry are present as plates of mince pies and mulled wine are passed round.

Diana has ensured that the Princes' early years are as full of wonder as her own were. Their

Christmas is the highlight of a year that can include visits to the London Dungeon, a ride in an army armoured tank, a visit to the police motorcycle unit in south London or the television comic Rod Hull and his ostrich Emu making a surprise birthday-party appearance.

The Princess's father, Earl Spencer, is her trump card. She still vividly remembers the astonishment she felt when a camel came ambling across the lawn towards her as she and her friends celebrated her seventh birthday. It was her father's closely guarded secret and he still has not lost the impresario's touch. One Christmas he turned the stately home into a wonderland with a huge Christmas tree, musical bears, an illuminated Santa Claus as well as a clown on stilts and a donkey and trap to greet the children when they arrived for tea. With a private visit to Father Christmas in the grotto at Harrods – Harry's wish one year was for a slice of Christmas cake – the boys are truly indulged by their mother.

For the adults the celebrations begin in earnest when the Queen hosts the Staff Party at Buckingham Palace. This takes place either the Tuesday or Thursday before Christmas Day and for once the footmen and the maids leave their uniforms in their wardrobes and join the royal family for an evening in the State Rooms.

A couple of days later, the Wales, their presents bought and wrapped, drive to Sandringham House where the royal family's Christmas celebrations follow a format that goes back to Queen Alexandra's days. She introduced the Danish custom of opening the presents on Christmas Eve and so the tradition has remained. A trestle table covered with a white linen cloth is erected in the Grand Saloon next to the Christmas tree. Strips of red ribbons and place cards in strict order of precedence indicate where the gifts should be placed.

Diana is unusual in that she chooses and buys many of the presents herself. Normally the network of valets and dressers goes into action during the autumn to find out what to buy for their royal employers. They prefer unusual or amusing rather than expensive presents. After all the biggest recurring headache must be what do you buy the Queen, the richest woman in the world?

Even Prince Charles finds it difficult. One year he delegated the task to Bobo MacDonald, the Queen's long-serving dresser. When she suggested that the Sovereign would like a new handbag, the Prince seized on the suggestion. Bobo went to a chic London store and purchased a lovely crocodile-skin model. However Charles, who has an annual income of £2 million ($3.4 million), was not best pleased when he was presented with the bill for £340 ($580). As one former member of staff remarked, 'When he saw the bill he nearly threw himself out of the window.'

When the royal family gather in the drawing room and open their presents it is not hard to see why he was so aggrieved. The wares on display hardly set the pulse racing. A compass for the Duke of Edinburgh, a rubber garden kneeling mat for Princess Alice, Duchess of Gloucester, and a funny hot-water bottle for the Duchess of Kent were just some of the offerings one year. While Diana's thoughts on receiving a green furry loo cover from her step-mother, Raine Spencer, are not recorded, her husband was pleased when he got a set of sable watercolour brushes. He was not too sure about the funny hat and pair of socks but his boys were delighted with their BMX bikes and new saddles.

It is as well that the royal family open their presents early as Christmas Day is hectic. The day starts at 7 a.m. with a gentle rap on the bedroom door from Diana's butler, Harold Brown, bearing the Christmas-morning tea tray. She quickly dresses before visiting her children in the royal nursery. At 8 o'clock the Princess and the rest of the royal family take Communion in the Saloon which is used as a temporary chapel. Traditionally the Queen, who is the Supreme Governor of the Church of England, never takes Communion in public.

Following Communion the royal adults gather in the dining room for breakfast. It is a serve-yourself affair with silver hotplates on the sideboard filled with bacon, eggs, kedgeree and sausages. There is no time to relax as the Princess prepares herself for the traditional Christmas service at Sandringham parish church which is situated about 800 yards from the main house. As they walk to church hundreds of wellwishers gather in the grounds.

The Queen Mother and Princess Margaret accept flowers from eager youngsters outside Sandringham church. Like Diana, Princess Margaret prefers the pleasures of the city to the rural delights of the Queen's Norfolk retreat.

After the hour-long service, which is relayed by loudspeaker to the crowds outside, the Princess emerges to be surrounded by dozens of youngsters who give her posies and Christmas cards. While the royal family are in church, their staff are hastily gulping down a couple of seasonal sherries as they put the finishing touches to the dining table.

As the royal family gather for lunch in the dining room, they are greeted by banks of cyclamen and poinsettias, specially grown in the Sandringham greenhouses for the occasion. For once lunch with the Queen is a totally informal occasion. As one long-suffering member of staff complained, 'It's like a madhouse, full of corgis and children running everywhere.' All the royal family, including the Queen, wear paper hats over their finery and indulge in good-natured horseplay. One year Diana, wearing a false plastic bosom over her gown, joined with Prince Andrew in attempting to steal Charles's trousers. Their antics were captured on film and the resulting Polaroid picture is now prominently displayed in Diana's photograph album.

Naturally the table is beautifully decorated with gold-edged Danish Flowers china, sparkling crystal, an ancient table decoration of Santa

The Princess and the Duchess of York return to Sandringham House following the annual Christmas church service.

Claus and his reindeer together with huge two-foot-long Christmas crackers, hand-made by Tom Smith's of Norwich. Inside these regal crackers are paper party hats, expensive trinkets like leather address books and china animals and, of course, rib-tickling jokes.

The meal is traditional festive fare and the royal family are served by liveried footmen and pages and enjoy Beluga caviar as a starter. While the rest of the world watches the Queen's traditional broadcast at 3 o'clock in the afternoon, the royal family feel no compulsion to see the programme. It is one of the many myths surrounding the Windsors that they all gather round to pass judgment on the monarch's performance. Instead they go for a walk around the grounds or play with their children.

In fact Diana has to supervise her children as her nanny and her dresser are absent. It is a tradition that staff from visiting Households see the Queen in her personal drawing room to receive a token Christmas gift such as a plastic pencil sharpener or a waste-paper basket. Yet these paltry trinkets are handed over with as much decorum as if the Queen was giving away her best jewels. Diana's dressers, Fay Appleby and Evelyn Dagley, are expected to wear their medals and white gloves while her nanny must wear her blue uniform. They curtsy twice, once on entering the room, a second time when they meet the Sovereign. As one recipient says, 'It's not the gift but the thought that the Queen has taken time on Christmas Day to see you which really counts.'

At 5 o'clock the royal family gather in the Saloon for tea with the Queen. Thinly cut cucumber sandwiches, chocolate cake and tea, poured by the monarch, are offered to the Princess and the rest of the family. 'Such a cosy meal,' says the Queen.

While Diana visits the nursery, the guests for 'Exiles' Night' arrive. This is a grand affair where all the deposed crowned heads of Europe join the Queen for dinner on Christmas evening. King Michael of Romania, ex-King Constantine of Greece, Prince Philip's Hanoverian relatives and Prince Tomislav of Yugoslavia swell the company who gather in the Grand Saloon. All the ladies are in their evening finery, the Princess wearing the Spencer tiara for the occasion.

'Diana and Fergie staged a chaotic version of the can-can.'

While this is a black-tie affair it did not stop Diana and Fergie introducing a note of levity on one occasion. In the first year of Fergie's marriage, when Christmas Court was still at Windsor Castle, they organized a disco in the Waterloo Room, so named because the portraits are of all the generals who fought in the battle. Their chaotic version of the can-can did not impress the Queen and the rest of the company and the discotheque soon petered out.

Boxing Day heralds the traditional Christmas shoot which follows a familiar pattern with a prompt 9.30 start, lunch in a remote church hall before everyone gathers in the Grand Saloon for tea with the children at 5 o'clock.

The evening pattern is broken occasionally by the showing of a film in the drawing room. As ever precedence rules, the Queen, the Queen Mother and the Duke of Edinburgh occupying the front seats. The movie, chosen by an equerry, does not always suit the Sovereign's taste. One evening they gathered to watch *The Taking of Pelham 123*, a violent drama starring Robert Shaw about the hijacking of a New York subway train. The language was as lurid as the action and the embarrassment among the Household grew with every expletive. Finally, with much tut-tutting, the Queen, the Queen Mother and a bishop walked out, duly followed by the rest of the Household. That equerry was never allowed to choose the film again.

Prince Charles is a man for whom familiarity, not the unexpected, breeds contentment and there is no more traditional sight than the youngest footman in royal service crossing the royal threshold of the front door on New Year's Eve. As the radio plays the chimes from Big Ben, he knocks on the door and enters, carrying a tray of drinks which he offers to the royal family. His reward is usually a miniature whisky with which to toast in the New Year.

As with other families the New Year is a time for looking and planning ahead, dreaming of longer days and warmer climes. While the public

wade through endless holiday brochures, the Windsors have already mapped out their destinations for the coming year. Invitations to visit an overseas country are often made years ahead by the host country. Planning a trip takes at least six months from the initial visit, where the Palace press officer, Scotland Yard bodyguard and possibly private secretary run through the proposed programme with a stopwatch and an eye for the media and security, to the moment when the Princess of Wales steps off the plane.

On most of her foreign visits, she is a couple of paces behind her husband, silently and attractively following in his wake. New York was different. It was her first major overseas visit in her own right. Ostensibly it was to attend the Welsh National Opera's first American performance of Verdi's *Falstaff*. In reality it was the chance for the Princess to make a personal impact on North America and to sell British goods in this vital market. On both counts the flying 44-hour trip was adjudged a success.

Preparation was the key. The Princess, in conjunction with her lady-in-waiting, Anne Beckwith-Smith, and Francis Cornish, from the British Embassy in Washington, organized an itinerary which deftly combined the cultural and commercial with Diana's interests in social problems. Her work with Aids in Britain – she made royal history by shaking the hands of a victim – was a natural springboard for a visit to an Aids centre in New York. While the Princess was convinced, Dr Margaret Heagarty who runs a children's Aids centre in Harlem needed some persuading. She has seen too many VIPs visit the centre with just one interest – publicity for themselves – and Cornish needed all his diplomatic charm to reassure the doctor that Diana was genuinely concerned, citing her work in Britain as part of her royal curriculum vitae.

Her initial doubts evaporated as she watched Diana cradle a number of terminally ill youngsters during a 90-minute tour of the pediatric unit. 'Our own royalty, whatever that is in democracy, has not done as much as you, anything so symbolic as you,' she told the Princess afterwards. 'Thank you for bringing life, youth and vitality to Harlem. God bless you.'

It was an emotional day for Diana who was still haunted on the Concorde flight home by

Variety is the spice which enlivens overseas tours. Diana's life on the royal road has seen her with a troupe of Nigerian dancers *(above)* and a pair of Indonesian girls in native costume *(right)*.

the vision of a seven-year-old she had cuddled. 'It was so sad,' she said. 'I think about how I held him in my arms. It was so moving.'

While she relaxed her emotional defences on the way to London, she was the epitome of compassionate professionalism during the visit. From the Aids centre she went directly to a reception for the Royal Academy of Music of which she is president. The chief administrator, John Bliss, who introduced her to stars like Bianca Jagger and Yoko Ono, was impressed by her composure. He recalls, 'She had just visited the Aids centre and seen dying children. It must have been emotionally exhausting. But she came into our reception and talked to people as if nothing had happened. None of us could believe how she could switch off. Her profession-alism is astonishing.'

Yet this is the same girl who sobbed her heart out in the back of a royal limousine in Leeds

'A royal tour is a combination of stultifying boredom, sublime settings and ridiculous red tape.'

following her first-ever visit to a hospice. 'She has come a long way since then,' notes John Bliss. 'She is a warm, thinking person and unlike so many English people in that she will touch people when she is talking or will reach out to shake hands. It means something to people.'

Certainly cynical New York was impressed. 'Bye bye sweet Di' ran the headlines while Yoko Ono, not noted for her admiration of the Establishment, commented, 'The British should consider themselves lucky to have such a beautiful and intelligent woman as their future queen.'

It is her willingness to adopt unpopular social issues, such as the heroin addicts she saw in Hong Kong and the lepers she met in Nigeria and Indonesia, which has been the proving of the Princess when she goes abroad. These days her foreign visits are short, sharp and with a point, which usually means highlighting a neglected problem close to her heart.

It was the very fact that New York had not given her the red-carpet treatment which impressed the Princess. Usually red tape and royalty go together much to the frustration and amusement of the Prince and Princess.

The attempts by zealous hosts to gloss over an untidy reality are noticed by the royal couple. As Charles says, 'I hate the smell of fresh paint. It sticks in my nose and makes me feel nauseous. Why do people paint everything when I am due somewhere?' Indeed one of the few services the media performed for the Prince and Princess was when they prevented a hotel manager painting the bedroom due to be used by Charles and Diana during a visit to Alice Springs in the Australian outback.

Early on in her royal career Diana became used to the elaborate flummery dreamed up by over-enthusiastic dignitaries. When she landed in Halifax, Nova Scotia, for her first visit to Canada she would have noticed large areas of bare earth which had been painted green to match the specially imported turf brought in to mark her regal progress. It was on the same tour that the captain of the Canadian destroyer accompanying the royal yacht *Britannia* ordered two men onto an iceberg to chip off a block of ice. The ice is an essential ingredient in the highly potent local brew called 'Screech' which the gallant captain wished to offer Diana.

This was merely a curtain raiser for the extravagance she experienced during her visits to the Middle East where the Princess was given several suites of jewellery, some still hidden in the royal vaults. In Saudi Arabia and Kuwait their generous hosts literally carpeted the desert with expensive Persian rugs so that the royal couple could enjoy a barbecue of whole roast lamb and other Middle Eastern delicacies.

Middle Eastern sheiks have a soft spot for the Princess. When she visited Oman she was given a sapphire and diamond necklace, earrings and bracelet by the Sultan while Prince Charles received a new Aston Martin sports car.

While their hospitality was lavish it paled by comparison with the excesses of one West African state. In 1990 the royal couple stayed for less than 24 hours in Cameroon but President Paul Biya rolled out rather more than the red carpet. He knew that the Princess enjoys tennis and swimming and so ordered the swimming pool in the President's guest house, where Charles and Diana spent one night, to be ripped out and replaced by an Olympic-sized version and a new clay tennis court to be laid.

A royal tour is a combination of stultifying boredom, sublime settings and ridiculous red tape. On the night of a banquet in Melbourne when Diana first wore her silver off-the-shoulder evening gown, she found herself in a very public predicament. Halfway through the meal the Princess, who was seated at the top table, wished to visit the bathroom. She made her excuses and departed, watched by hundreds of fellow guests. The nearest bathroom was located just outside. That however was not good enough for the Australian security guards who insisted on taking her to the 11th floor which in their jargon was 'a sterile zone'. She recalled afterwards, 'It was so embarrassing, I had to keep crossing and recrossing my legs all the way.'

However, many of the funniest incidents in the royal roadshow occur off stage. During a visit to Canada there was a scene straight from the script of a French farce. Prince Charles's usual routine is to sleep in total darkness which means that in the morning his valet runs his bath, lays out his clothes and quietly wishes him 'Good morning, Your Royal Highness' in the dark. This is fine at Kensington Palace where servants know the layout of the bedroom but poses problems when the Prince is staying elsewhere. On this occasion Charles had an enormous suite in a hotel. Promptly at 6.30 a.m. the royal valet tapped on the Prince's door, entered and performed his duties. Then he discreetly retired quietly closing the door behind him. To his horror the servant discovered that he had inadvertently walked into the suite's huge walk-in wardrobe. Vainly he tried to open the door but to his dismay it remained firmly closed. Gently he tapped on the wardrobe door, hoping to attract the Prince's attention. 'Go away,' said Charles as he attempted to slumber. The knocking persisted. Charles, irritated at having his early morning reverie disturbed, then said tetchily, 'What is it? What is it?'

'Could you open the door, sir?' came the plaintive reply. With much grumpy huffing and puffing the Prince put on his towelling robe and opened the door, only to find an empty corridor. The Prince, by now as bewildered as he was annoyed, then heard the disembodied voice from the wardrobe. 'I'm in here, sir.' Charles effected his manservant's release and for days afterwards the incident was the talk of the party.

While light-hearted moments liven up a tour, these visits are working trips with a serious commercial and political purpose in mind. The Wales' stay in Hong Kong, for example, was designed to reassure the community that Britain had not forgotten its obligations to the colony even though the take-over by Communist China in 1997 dominated every conversation. A recent trip to Nigeria helped strengthen the commercial ties with this vital oil-exporting nation.

Wherever possible these visits are over in a working week so that Diana can return home to see her sons. The joyous homecoming does not always go to plan. When she arrived back from a tour of the Far East, Prince William bounced into the room and demanded, 'Where is my present?' Then he raced to the nursery leaving a crestfallen Princess in his wake. Of course, he got a present; the Princess always collects armfuls of tee-shirts and toys for the boys when she is on tour.

Presents loom large when the Princess returns to Highgrove, especially following tours undertaken in the spring. When she opens her mail she usually finds a clutch of invitations to weddings. Indeed the Princess attends so many Society weddings during the summer season that there are few smart drawing rooms in Kensington, Chelsea or Fulham which do not boast a leather-framed photograph of the Princess sitting with the wedding party.

For the wedding of her brother, Viscount Charles Althorp to model Victoria Lockwood, she agreed to let Prince Harry be a page boy. Ever since he nearly upstaged the Duchess of York at her wedding at Westminster Abbey, Prince William has become used to his Saturday-afternoon role as a page boy. In fact, when the

The summer season is Diana's busiest time. She is a frequent guest at Society weddings although her sons do not seem to share her enthusiasm. Prince Harry was distinctly bemused by the Cavalier outfit he wore for the wedding of Diana's brother, Viscount Althorp, and Victoria Lockwood *(below)* while William obviously felt his pink braces were no joke *(below left)*.

The Queen Mother and the Princess acknowledge the cheers of the crowd as the royal carriage procession drives along the course at Ascot. As far as Diana is concerned the racing comes a poor second to the enjoyment of meeting friends and soaking up the atmosphere at this fashionable Society event.

boys watch the video of their parents' wedding they cannot understand why they were not present.

While the Princess likes to buy her sons new outfits, invariably designed by Catherine Walker, to complement the bride's dress she makes it a rule never to wear anything new herself so that she does not detract from the bride's big day. The day before the wedding she usually telephones the bride to wish her well and steady her nerves. 'Marriage? I can highly recommend it,' is a phrase which frequently falls from her lips. While the local police force is informed that the Princess will be a wedding guest, security is usually low-key. Diana slips in late accompanied by her detective and takes a seat in any vacant pew. 'We were halfway through the wedding service when I realized that I was standing next to the Princess of Wales,' recalls one guest. She joins the party for the wedding photographs and reception afterwards before making her way back to Kensington Palace.

The Princess has several godchildren and keeps a weather eye on them all. Among them are George Frost, the son of the television personality David Frost, the Duke of Westminster's daughter, Lady Edwina Grosvenor, and Lord Downpatrick, the Earl of St Andrews'

The Princess, seated next to the Duke of Kent, takes an active interest in the Centre Court battles at Wimbledon. She played a charity doubles match with champion Steffi Graf who she hopes will coach Prince William.

son. It all means a busy social whirl, perhaps the most enjoyable time of the year for the Princess. The summer season is a time for involvement with people at the many social gatherings.

She is a familiar figure in the royal box at Wimbledon's Centre Court, taking friends like Kate Menzies and Catherine Soames for a day out in the sunshine. As a keen tennis player she revels in the action and was disappointed when the call of royal duty forced her to miss seeing Steffi Graf in action in the ladies' final in 1989.

However the pinnacle of the summer social season is the four-day royal meeting at Ascot racecourse. While not regarded by serious punters as the premier flat race meeting of the year, it is undoubtedly the major royal event. For most of June the Queen is in residence at Windsor Castle and during Ascot week she hosts a house party where the Princess is able to invite her friends to enjoy a very civilized day at the races. It was during one house party when Prince Andrew's romance with Sarah Ferguson started in earnest as they enjoyed teasing conversation over a plateful of chocolate profiteroles. Indeed Sarah was Diana's guest. On another occasion Diana and Fergie were nicknamed the 'merry wives of Windsor' when they were photographed prodding the bottom of their friend, Lulu Blacker, with their rolled umbrellas.

While the Princess stays at the Castle, invited guests only spend the day with the Queen, arriving at midday and leaving their cars in the castle forecourt. Guests are formally introduced to a line-up of the royal family by the Queen's senior equerry, Blair Stewart-Wilson. As pages in semi-state livery offer guests a glass of champagne or Pimm's, the royal family and their guests mingle and chat before going in for luncheon in the Waterloo Room. There is a printed seat plan and after guests have found their places, they stand behind their chairs until the Queen is seated.

Conversation follows a certain protocol. During the first course of fish, everyone speaks to the person on their left, for the meat course and dessert they turn to the right. As one guest recalls, 'It is a very relaxed atmosphere despite the fact that there are endless footmen around. You're not so nervous that you are thinking, "Oh my god, I'm going to be sick."'

The sense of ease is deceptive because everyone has to be safely inside their limousines by 1.35 p.m. and drive to the Ascot Gate of Windsor Great Park where they change into carriages, leaving at 1.45 p.m. for the traditional drive down the course.

On a sunny day, with the ladies in their finery and the men in their top hats and tails, this timeless setting is reminiscent of the famous 'Ascot Opening Day' scene from Diana's favourite musical, *My Fair Lady*.

The similarity between Eliza Doolittle's progress into Society and her own royal progress is not lost on the Princess as she sits in an open carriage waving to the cheering crowds. The pages of her diaries show how she has developed from an uncertain teenager into a lively, independent and composed future queen.

The metropolitan Princess has come of age.

The pages of Diana's diary reveal a composed yet lively young woman who has truly come of age.

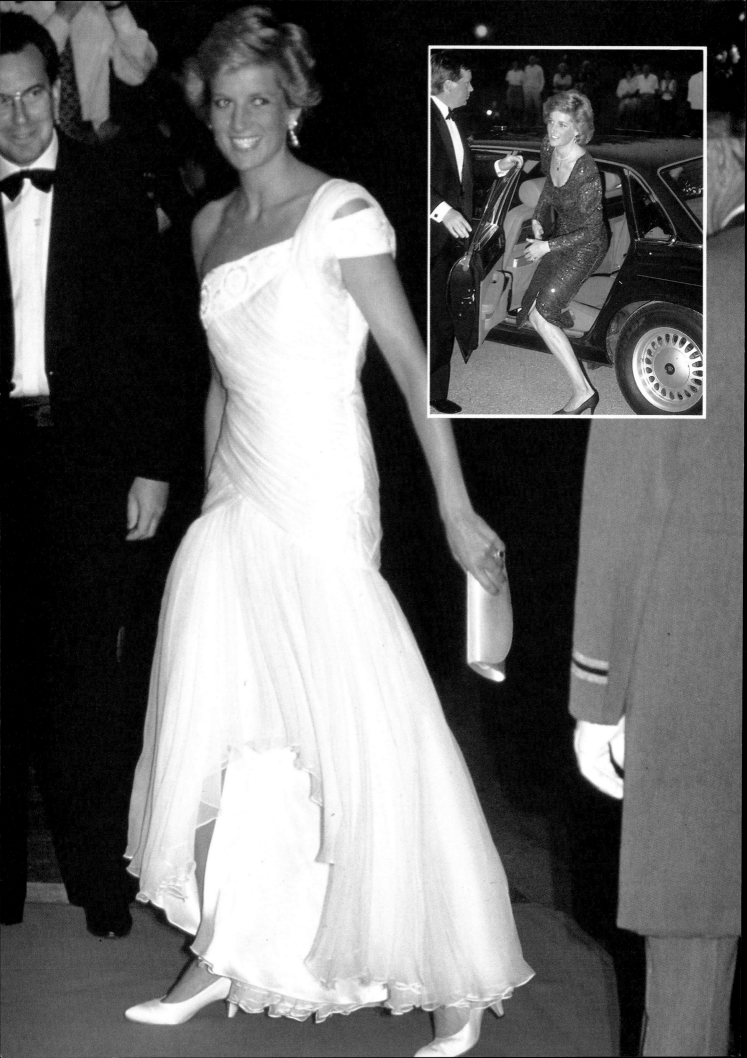

The Wardrobe of the Princess of Wales

The Princess of Wales and her wardrobe is a subject which fascinates many people. Since her engagement in February 1981 the Princess has built up an extensive range of fashions to fulfil her many public engagements which can range from a formal banquet in the White House to a visit to a playgroup. While the Foreign Office gives her a dress allowance for her overseas tours, the Princess has paid for the majority of her wardrobe from her own resources – she receives an allowance from the Duchy of Cornwall estates and has her own trust fund. So just what does she own and how much is her wardrobe worth?

Margaret Holder, contributing editor to *Royalty* magazine, has analysed the wardrobe of the Princess of Wales in the decade since the engagement in 1981. The outfits and accessories included have either been photographed or the details made public.

At the same time, over the last decade, the Princess has acquired a considerable private wardrobe which includes foreign designers such as Kenzo, Valentino and Gianni Versace. The value of her private wardrobe was estimated following extensive interviews with staff from her favourite stores and designers. It is worth noting that, unlike other members of the royal family, the Princess does not have a reputation of asking for trade prices when she buys her private clothes.

In all, Margaret Holder estimates that in the ten years since 1981 the Princess has spent a little over £1.1 million ($1.9 million) on her wardrobe, a total which includes £200,000 ($340,000) for her private purchases. This is how it breaks down:

When the Princess attends charity galas or first nights she has more than 90 evening gowns worth almost £200,000 ($340,000) to choose from.

Wardrobe	Total (£)	Total ($)
Evening gowns:		
91 at £2,000 ($3,400)	£182,000	($309,400)
4 at £4,000 ($6,800)	£16,000	($27,200)
Tuxedos: 2 at £1,200 ($2,040)	£2,400	($4,080)
Dresses: 176 at £1,000 ($1,700)	£176,000	($299,200)
Suits: 178 at £1,250 ($2,125)	£222,500	($378,250)
Coats: 54 at £1,000 ($1,700)	£54,000	($91,800)
Hats and mantilla:		
141 at £200 ($340)	£28,200	($47,940)
Blouses/shirts:		
71 at £250 ($425)	£17,750	($30,175)
Skirts: 29 at £200 ($340)	£5,800	($9,860)
Trousers/culottes:		
25 at £200 ($340)	£5,000	($8,500)
Sweaters: 28 at £100 ($170)	£2,800	($4,760)
Jackets: 29 at £150 ($255)	£4,350	($7,395)
Shoes: 350 at £100 ($170)	£35,000	($59,500)
Boots/ski boots:		
12 at £150 ($255)	£1,800	($3,060)
Bags: 200 at £125 ($212)	£25,000	($42,500)
Ski/sportswear	£1,350	($2,295)
Fur jacket	£5,000	($8,500)
Belts/gloves/muffs	£5,000	($8,500)
Nightwear	£20,000	($34,000)
Underwear	£13,500	($22,950)
Tights	£6,750	($11,475)
Fake jewels	£4,500	($7,650)
Robes/uniforms	£3,500	($5,950)
Wedding ensemble	£30,000	($51,000)
Other robes (given)	£50,000	($85,000)
Sub total	**£918,200**	**($1,560,940)**
Private wardrobe	£200,000	($340,000)
GRAND TOTAL	**£1,118,200**	**($1,900,940)**
Annual expenditure	**£124,244**	**($211,216)**
Monthly expenditure	**£10,354**	**($17,601)**
Weekly expenditure	**£2,389**	**($4,062)**

The Astrological Chart
of the Princess of Wales

Born on 1 July 1961, the Princess of Wales is in many ways a typical Cancerian. Her love of children and concern for the welfare of others comes from this nurturing moon sign, as does a strong sense of loyalty and belief in old-fashioned values. Cancer is the most emotional and introverted sign in the zodiac, so she is extremely sensitive and easily hurt and she has had to learn to deal with being constantly in the public eye, something which does not come naturally to her.

However, Diana's ascendant or rising sign (the zodiac sign rising over the eastern horizon at the moment of birth) is outgoing Sagittarius and this tempers some of her Cancerian characteristics. Sagittarius is a very positive fire sign, full of the spirit of adventure and very broad minded. Cancer on the other hand, is a water sign, so she is something of an emotional yo-yo. She goes from extremes of high to low with nothing in between. She can be impulsive and she tends to make decisions of the heart rather than the head.

Happily, the Moon was in Aquarius when Diana was born and that provides a balance in her birthchart which helps her to avoid the more extreme tendencies. Aquarius is an emotionally detached, logical sign, capable of viewing situations with great objectivity. It is also the sign of the humanitarian, so she is very aware of human rights issues, and places great importance on the freedom of the individual. This moon position gives her a need for a great deal of personal space. That is unusual for a Cancerian; normally they do not like to be alone, or to do anything without their partner. Diana's Moon gives her an independence of spirit which demands that she be seen as an individual within the matrimonial unit. She welcomes those times when she can pursue her own interests, and sees nothing wrong with the

fact that those interests do not coincide with her husband's. Therefore, the fact that Charles and Diana seem to spend a lot of their leisure time apart should not in itself be taken as indicative of problems within the marriage.

In spite of the fact that the Prince of Wales was born under fixed, possessive Scorpio, Sagittarius is strongly emphasized in his birthchart. This means that in certain respects he too is a free spirit and he would resent a partner who tried to tie him down too much. There are times when he is irritated by Diana's independent streak but in the main, it is something he respects and will value.

The comparison between the birthcharts of Charles and Diana reveals a great deal about their relationship. It is certainly not a dull partnership. There are many dynamic aspects which indicate a strong sexual attraction and a deep emotional attachment. But there is a lot of tension there too and they do annoy each other quite easily. When there is tension between them, Diana's instinctive reaction is to withdraw and behave with coolness. This can be very frustrating for Charles because he cannot judge her reactions or feelings.

The marriage has been particularly difficult for both of them in the latter half of the 1980s. Charles has been undergoing a considerable transformation under the influence of Pluto. He has an enormous power within him and he feels driven to use it. This, he feels is HIS time. He must now make his mark.

Such deep, personal change is of necessity a selfish business. Anyone undergoing this kind of challenge could be forgiven for being rather withdrawn. Apart from anything else, it uses up an immense amount of energy and it is an all-consuming business. Undoubtedly, this has not made Charles easy to live with.

Meanwhile, Diana's chart indicates that she has been feeling weighed down with responsibility. Saturn is the planet of limitation and it has been sitting in a very sensitive part of her chart. This has probably made her feel rather misunderstood, and it has made it difficult for her to communicate her feelings to others – especially Charles. So both of them have been living in their private worlds and dealing with their respective pain in a solitary fashion.

Diana is now coming out of that phase. 1991 is the year in which Saturn returns to the position it was in when she was born. Astrologically, this is known as the age of emotional maturity, so it is growing-up time for her. Usually, a greater degree of self-confidence follows the Saturn return, plus a strong sense of direction. This is the time when Diana should gain a realistic sense of self-worth, and her priorities will alter.

By nature, Diana is an extravagant, sensual person. She likes the good things in life and she places a lot of importance on material things. This is one of the areas where she is likely to change during the 1990s. She is entering a more serious, cerebral phase in which she is developing strong views and beliefs about a wide range of issues. In making self-deprecating remarks like 'I'm as thick as a plank' Diana does not do herself justice. Her chart shows her to be quite intelligent and communicative, with an absorbent mind and an excellent memory. She will become more intellectual as she gets older. Her awareness of matters such as environmental issues is likely to become broader. During this process, she will come more into line with the beliefs, causes and interests which Charles espouses and this will provide a new common bond between them.

For Charles, a thinking woman is an attractive woman. He places much more emphasis on the mind than the body. An underdeveloped mind which lacks conviction bores him, no matter how physically attractive the person might be. It would be unjust to suggest that Diana falls into the underdeveloped category, but inevitably her youth and the age gap between them has caused a communication problem. Charles may well have developed a habit of dismissing Diana's views and ideas.

There is now a wonderful opportunity for all that to change. Currently, there are very good connections between their charts. The Moon in Diana's map is very close to Mercury in Charles's.

This indicates that she will be able to respond to his thoughts and feelings at the deepest level, intuitively understanding what he thinks and feels.

In turn, Charles can now discover the wonderfully supportive sympathetic elements his partner has to offer. That could bring this troubled couple closer than they have ever been and a third child could be the result. September of 1991 is the most likely time for Diana to give birth.

There has been a great deal of speculation about whether Charles will ever accede to the throne. Since Pluto will make a close connection with Charles's Sun in 1992, many astrologers feel that he will not.

Close examination of several royal charts does indicate that this will be a critical time for the entire family. There are several possibilities and it is impossible to be definitive in predicting the final outcome. The options are as follows:

1. The Queen's chart indicates that an illness may become serious and could result in her requiring surgery. There is also an indication of bereavement in her map. Such a situation could cause her to abdicate in favour of Charles. Certainly, Diana's chart for the beginning of 1992 indicates a rise in status and a change of home.

2. Charles will die as a result of an accident. This has been predicted by many astrologers, based on the fact that Pluto will make a close connection with his Sun. Indeed, this will mark an ending of some kind, but not necessarily in the literal sense. While Diana, William and Harry all have indications of an inheritance in their charts, there is no evidence of such a close bereavement, so this negative, fatalistic forecast should be treated as a definite 'maybe'.

3. The final option is that Charles will have a brainstorm as a final part of his personal transformation. This could cause him to leave his wife and children and abnegate his current responsibilities. This is entirely possible, but it would be reasonable to expect this to be reflected in Diana's chart. Far from a rise in status, embarrassment and humiliation would surely be indicated, as would a sudden break in a relationship. Again, this is not the case. However, Libra is prominent in the charts of both William and Harry. Libra is the sign of balance and this could suggest that the boys will be a factor in bargaining between their parents.

There is no doubt that the new decade will be one of profound change for the Princess of Wales.

MARTINE DELAMERE

Acknowledgements

I am indebted to the officials of the charities associated with the Princess of Wales for their insights and observations. In particular I would like to thank Sister Barbara, Passage Day Centre; John Bliss, Royal Academy of Music; David French, Relate; Valerie Howarth, Childline; Vivienne Parry, Birthright; Les Rudd, Turning Point; Roger Singleton, Barnardo's; and Jimmy Savile.

In the world of fashion my thanks to David Sassoon and Gina Fratini for their advice and sketches, as well as Murray Arbeid, Paul Costelloe, Victor Edelstein, Rifat Ozbek, and Philip Somerville.

I would also like to thank Sally Armstrong, Wensley Clarkson, Francis Cornish, Joseph Corvo, Barbara Daly, Martine Delamere, Janet Filderman, Lubna Hussain, Nigel Milne, Bangie and Beryl Pringle, Rosemary Verey, and Dr Peter Wilde for their contributions. My gratitude also to Sylvia Munro for releasing the diaries of the Princess's former dancing teacher, the late Lilian Snipp.

Numerous friends, present and previous royal employees, and those who supply goods and services to the royal family were interviewed on a confidential basis. While respecting their anonymity my gratitude to them is nonetheless heartfelt.

Special thanks also, to my researcher Margaret Holder, contributing editor to *Royalty* magazine, whose indefatigable efforts uncovered numerous gems. As ever, thanks to my publisher Michael O'Mara for his encouragement and my wife Lynne for her forbearance.

ANDREW MORTON, JUNE 1990

Picture Acknowledgements
All photographs by Nunn Syndication with the exception of the following:
Alpha: 37, 76, 80, 81; Barnardo's: 9 *(bottom)*, 45, 91 *(bottom)*, 92; Lionel Cherruault: 51 *(top)*; Gina Fratini: 46 *(bottom right)*; Tim Graham: 18–19 *(bottom)*, 36 *(top and bottom)*, 40, 41, 46 *(bottom left)*, 57, 59, 63, 67, 74, 87, 108; Anwar Hussein: 43, 52, 79; JS Library: 68 *(bottom)*; Julian Parker: 44 *(left)*; Photographers International: 77, 83 *(bottom right)*; Ronald Reagan Presidential Library: 83 *(top and bottom left)*; Rex Features: 33 *(top)*, 71; David Sassoon: 46 *(top right)*.